Brewing Beers Like Those You Buy

DAVE LINE

NEXUS SPECIAL INTERESTS

Reviser's note: Some of the ingredients and equipment originally recommended by Dave Line are no longer appropriate, or as easy to obtain, as they were when the book was written. I have revised the text as little as possible in updating it. The actual recipes the author suggested have not been altered, except for a few instances where ingredients (such as glucose chips) are no longer available. In those cases, what I believe to be the nearest suitable ingredient has been substituted.

Due to brewery takeovers and amalgamations, and changes in demand, some beers are no longer on sale. But they are beers worth remembering, and the recipes have been left in. Where these have been identified, I have added a small symbol (⊞) to the heading, so you won't spend fruitless hours searching for the original beer for comparison.

Dave Line was probably the most skilled, innovative, and articulate home brewer of his time; I hope he would approve of my revisions — after a pint or two!

Roy Ekins

DEDICATION
To Sheila and Robert

Photographs by Paul Ekins

Published by
Nexus Special Interests Ltd.
Nexus House,
Boundary Way,
Hemel Hempstead,
Herts
HP2 7ST

First published 1978
Reprinted 1978, 1979, 1980 (twice), 1981,
1982 (three times), 1983, 1984, 1988, 1989, 1991, 1993
This revised edition 1995
Reprinted 1997

ISBN 1-85486-125-5

Printed and bound in Great Britain by
Biddles Ltd, Guildford & King's Lynn

THANKS

The concept of 'Brewing Beers Like Those You Buy' generated a tremendous enthusiasm from all those who knew about the project.

Space will not permit me to repeat and record my thanks individually to all the people who have helped. Even so, I would like to thank collectively the friends throughout the country and indeed many parts of the world who sent information and samples of beers for analysis which has enabled me to present such a balanced selection of beers for you to brew. Many of the regional draught beers were found at Beer Festivals organised by the Campaign for Real Ale and I would like to thank the organisers and fellow members of the movement for their help and co-operation with the collection of these samples

My particular thanks must, however, go to the commercial brewers and the brewing industry itself. Much of the recipe formulation was done from information freely given by the breweries who are proud to divulge the quality of their ingredients and practices.

Finally my thanks go to my wife Sheila for typing the manuscript and for her patience with my brewing activities and the chaos that reigned in our household during the writing of this book.

Dave Line

CONTENTS

INTRODUCTION

THE ANSWER TO THE BEER DRINKER'S DREAM!

'BREWING BEERS LIKE THOSE YOU BUY' gives you all the know-how to brew a beer just like your favourite pub tipple, but at a fraction of the price across the bar.

Great names like Draught Bass, Worthington 'E', Carlsberg, Double Diamond, Guinness and Schlitz take on a new meaning. Over one hundred famous beers selected from all over the world are included and the fullest details are given to ensure that anyone, even without any previous knowledge of brewing, can produce a beer which will do justice in flavour and quality to the original brew.

Flick through the pages and see how many of your favourite beers are included. And then reflect that you brew a gallon of it for the price of a pint in the pub. The methods are simplicity itself and even the cost of a fully equipped home brewery can be recouped in two brewing sessions. Indeed, using normal kitchen equipment and utensils, some recipes can be brewed using additional containers costing less than a pint of beer!

Get started now and be supping your own in a few weeks time.

CHAPTER 1

BREWING BEERS LIKE THOSE YOU BUY

IT took twenty years of brewing, experimenting and drinking by enthusiastic amateurs to bring the craft of home brewing to the stage where we can produce beers to match the quality of our commerical counterparts. Given the ingredients and the methods it is hardly surprising that amateur brewers will want to try to brew a beer like their favourite pub tipple. 'Brewing Beers Like Those You Buy' sets out to help them in this quest.

The book does not tell how to brew exact copies of particular beers, but it is as the title states, about brewing beers *like* commercial versions. Using home brew methods it is impossible to turn out the same beer as a large brewery. What we can do is emulate your favourite beer with a fair degree of success. Similar flavour, strength and colour can be achieved and in such a way that you may end up liking the home brew version better than the original.

I must clearly state that none of the recipes given in the book list (or intentionally list) the exact brewing ingredients and procedures of the quoted beer. Even although I have been entrusted with the complete formulation and brewing techniques for many beers, it would be pointless duplicating them here. I have tried many times to brew to commercial recipes and in nearly every case the brew turned out a disappointing imitation. To achieve the best results it was often necessary to change the basic ingredients or even add others.

The limitations of home brew equipment and availability of certain items has generally meant my formulations include more malt adjuncts and sweeteners. Being technical, to give an example, home brewed beer tends to ferment more than commercial equivalents, giving a stronger, more alcoholic brew with a drier taste for the same starting ingredients. We cannot successfully filter out the excess yeast nor control the storage temperature to limit this prolonged fermentation, so my brews may have different starting gravities and contain artificial sweeteners to help restore the balance in the finished beer.

Quoting brand names is the clearest way of identifying beer characteristics. Originally the book was just going to include a full selection of types and flavours of beers. My recipe for a 'strong, full malty flavoured bitter with delicious well balanced hop bite' applied to Adnams 'Southwold Bitter', Eldridge Pope's 'Royal Oak' and Gales 'H.S.B.' for starters. And this was confusing because these beers have their subtle differences, and I know people that love two out of the three, but hate the other!

I cannot describe an identity for a particular beer any better than the breweries can themselves, so I have accepted the easy way out. If someone wants to brew a strong ale like Gibbs Mew's 'The Bishops Tipple', they know what they want and so do I. And this is what 'Brewing Beers Like Those You Buy' is all about.

BEER LIST

LAGERS
Skol, Carling Black Label, Carlsberg Special Brew, Konig, Harp, Long Life, Tennents, Tuborg, Heineken, Budweiser, Colt 45, Schlitz, Castlemaine Bitter, Fosters, Resch, Southwark Bitter, Stella Artois, Pilsner Urquell, Kronenbourg Export, Hansa Export, Lowenbrau, Grolsch, Perroni, Diekirch, Zywiec Tatra, Tiger, San Miguel, Hurlimann Sternbrau.

LIGHT ALES
Toby Light, Ind Coope, Sainsburys, Newcastle Amber Ale, Whitbreads.

PALE ALES
Worthington White Label, Greene King Pale Ale, McEwans IPA, Wee Willie, Lion Ale

REAL ALES
Fullers ESB, Adnams Southwold, Arkells BBB Bitter, Arkells Kingsdown Ale, Draught Bass, Brakspears Special Bitter, Courages Directors Bitter, Courages Barnsley Bitter,

Courages Best Bitter, Davenports Bitter, Donnington ASB Bitter, Eldridge Pope 'Royal Oak', Fullers London Pride, Gales H.S.B., Gibb Mew Bishops Tipple, Greene King Abbot Ale, Hall & Woodhouse Badger Best Bitter, Harveys Best Bitter, Hook Norton Old Bill Dark Ale, Ind Coope Burton Ale, King & Barnes PA Bitter, King & Barnes Mild Ale, King & Barnes Sussex Old Ale, Marstons Pedigree Bitter, Mitchell & Butler DPA Bitter, Morland Best Bitter, Morland Mild Ale, Morrells Varsity Bitter, Paines E.G. Bitter, Palmers I.P.A., Ruddles County, Samuel Smiths Old Brewery Bitter, Shepherd Neames Best Bitter, Tetleys Bitter, Theakstons Old Peculier, Theakstons Best Bitter, Tolly Cobbold Bitter, Ushers P.A., Wadworths 6X Bitter, Websters Pennine Bitter, Whitbreads Pompey Royal, Whitbreads Trophy Bitter, Youngs Special Bitter.

KEG BEERS
Worthington 'E', Draught John Courage, Tavern Keg, Double Diamond, Yorkshire Bitter, Ben Trumans Export, Watneys Special Bitter, Watneys Starlight, Watneys Special Mild, Whitbread Tankard, Tartan Keg.

BROWN ALES
Arkells Brown Jack, Greene King, Newcastle, Manns.

STOUTS
Palmers, Watneys Cream Label, Mackeson, Castle Milk Stout.

BARLEY WINES AND STRONG ALES
Arkells Kingsdown Ale, Courages 'Imperial Russian Stout', Eldridge Popes 'Thomas Hardy Ale', Gales 'Prize Old Ale', Greene King Strong Pale Ale, Greene King Suffolk Strong Ale, King & Barnes 'Sussex Old Ale', Wadworths 'Old Timer', Chimay.

14

CHAPTER 2

GETTING STARTED

HOME brewing is backed by a mature industry in Britain with hundreds of retail outlets catering for our needs in equipment, ingredients and literature on the subject. Because there is such a wealth of information about, I decided to make 'Brewing Beers Like Those You Buy' basically a recipe book, so you will not find a lot of brewing technicalities in the text—just sufficient to enable you to brew successfully. However, if after brewing some of these delicious beers you want to know some of the theory as to why they taste so good, then consult my first book, 'The Big Book of Brewing' which covers all aspects of home brewing. Do not forget, though, to raise your glass and toast your thanks to the commercial brewers who created the beers in the first place.

WHAT IS IN BEER?

Malt. Gives flavour, strength and aroma.
Hops. Imparts bitterness to balance the maltliness.
Sugar. Gives strength and sweetness.
Adjuncts. Other cereals sometimes used for economy and flavour.
Yeast. Converts the sugar into alcohol and carbon dioxide gas.
Water. Even the stronger beers contain 90% water.

INGREDIENTS NEEDED

The list of ingredients which can be, and are used in brewing is quite incredible. Indeed, even the traditional malt, hops and yeast can be processed, packaged and presented in a form which can baffle a newcomer to brewing. Go into any large home brew stockist and see the hundreds of different items covering ingredients and brewing 'aids'—it's no wonder beginners get confused and embarrassed.

I intend to save you experiencing these problems by briefly

describing the ingredients used in this book and why they are used.

Pale Malt Grains

Beer is produced by the action of yeast on a sugary flavoured solution. Most of this sweet solution (called wort) is obtained by processing malted barley grains, as will be shown later. Home brew shops stock these grains in a whole or crushed form. To be processed in the home they must be crushed and as the degree of crushing is critical, I would recommend not purchasing the grains whole. CRUSHED PALE MALT contains the light stone coloured husks and the white powdery interiors. Pale Malt represents the main weight of dry ingredients and cost in beer production and it is worth investing in a bulk purchase (say 50 kg.) arrangement with your home brew shop.

Lager Malt Grains

Lager malt looks very similar to pale malt and is used, surprise, surprise, for brewing lager! You need to get side by side samples to detect the lighter roasting of the lager malt. Looks are not everything, and lager malt is not a substitute for pale because different brewing techniques are required.

Roasted Grains

Barley, whether raw or malted, can be roasted and burnt to varying degrees to provide a useful means of colouring and flavouring beer. Only small quantities ($\frac{1}{4}\%$–10%) of the total malt content are normally required. From a golden colour to black, the range goes through crystal malt, amber malt, brown malt, chocolate malt, roast barley to black malt. All these grains require crushing before use, but as the degree of crushing is not critical the grain can be purchased whole if desired and cracked at home in a coffee mill or grinder. If you have got to resort to thumping it with a mallet or chasing it with a rolling pin in your attempts to crush it at home, save yourself the effort and buy it already done.

Malt Extract

The success of modern home brewing can be largely attributed to the availability of malt extract syrups. Although malt extract is a sticky dirty brown coloured substance it also presents the main beer ingredient as a very convenient manageable product that cuts down on brewing time; an important consideration for many following the hobby in their spare

16

time. Basically, an extract is mashed out of barley malt and then the liquid is concentrated to about one tenth of its original volume. Also sold as a powder; use 4/5th the quantity.

Barley Syrup

Barley syrup is similar to malt extract and can be used as a direct substitute. Whereas the extract is produced by the traditional brewing practice of mashing, the barley syrup form achieves the required conversion of starch to usable sugars by other chemical processes.

Wheat Malt

Wheat can be malted like barley but not with the same degree of success. Small quantities are used in the brew to assist the production of foam in the poured beer. A nice frothy head and a generous lacing of foam afterwards is some drinkers' guide to quality. BREWING FLOUR is this malt with the husks removed.

Flaked Maize

Flaked maize is, and looks like, small yellow cornflakes. It is a cheap, easy to use malt substitute popular with English and American breweries. The 'corn' flavour imparted is often the predominant characteristic of some beers.

Flaked Rice

Just as effective as a cheap source of extract, flaked rice gives strength without colour and is an ideal adjunct for delicately flavoured lagers. Being readily available in supermarkets it is especially cheap if you can swing the cost on to your wife's shopping budget!

Flaked Barley

Barley Flakes improve the head retention, body and flavour in beer. Dark beers can tolerate a higher proportion of this adjunct than light beers which can tend to remain cloudy through suspended protein matter.

Torrefied Barley

Torrefied barley is barley where the grain has been enlarged like the breakfast cereal 'Puffed Wheat'. Make your own in a lidded pan, like popcorn.

Sugar

Commercial brewers rarely use pure white household sugar—it's too expensive and also it has had all of the desirable luscious flavouring substances refined out.

Combinations of Invert and dark sugars, molasses, treacles and caramels are made up to suit each brewery's requirements. At our end of the trade these sugars are more expensive than the white, but don't be tempted to substitute for the latter because you will ruin the flavour balance of the beer.

Many beers are sweet or possess residual sweetness. For simplicity, I recommend using saccharin tablets, the type where one tablet has equivalent sweetness to one teaspoonful (5 ml.) of white sugar. Instead of saccharine, you can substitute an equal number of teaspoons of Aspartame (Nutrasweet, Canderel), or use its stabilised homebrew equivalent Vinsweet. GLUCOSE CHIPS and INVERT SUGAR are not now readily available. You can make your own Invert sugar by boiling a kilo of white granulated (or brown if in the recipe) sugar with a teaspoon of citric acid for a few minutes, and neutralising the residual acid afterwards. For the small gain in fermentation time it is not worth the bother. Much better is to buy Brewing Sugar (Malto-dextrin) from your homebrew specialist, and use this in the same quantities. LACTOSE is a non-fermenting sugar used mainly for sweetening brown ales and sweet stouts.

Hops

The hop is a perennial bine that grows twenty feet or more like a giant runner bean plant with a left handed thread. Only the dried female flowers of hop plant are used in brewing and these are best described as looking like reject Brussels sprouts. In the beer they impart a beautiful aroma, flavour and bitterness to balance the body and sweetness of the malt. No wonder malt and hops are called the perfect partnership.

About a dozen varieties of hops are available to the home brew trade and they have delightful names like Goldings, Fuggles and Bullion.

Hop pellets are becoming popular in home brewing and can be substituted in all recipes after making allowances for concentration of goodness. The availability of some lesser known types of hops is erratic in home brew circles and it may be necessary to find substitutes. For Bramling Cross and Whitbread Goldings (W.G.V.) substitute Hallertauer.

ISOMERISED HOP EXTRACTS are concentrated, processed extracts of hop bittering resins. They do not need to be boiled and can be added after the fermentation to adjust the bitterness level in the finished beer. The flavour is generally inferior to that achieved by traditional hopping techniques so only small final adjustments are normally used to ensure a consistent product.

Water

Beer is nearly all water. So do not bother to impart this gem of knowledge to your landlord, because even if he appreciates over 90% of what he sells you is water you will not be thanked for ensuring all his customers know this fact as well!

For most purposes, water is a pretty inert substance; in its purest form a tasteless, colourless, neutral liquid. Water from the natural sources in rivers, wells and public supply systems contains minute quantities of dissolved mineral salts which can influence brewing processes to a marked degree. Chlorine is added to most public water supplies, and reacts with the hops to produce an unpleasant medicinal smell and taste (TCP). It is advisable to use a water filter or boil all water used for brewing, for about ten minutes.

Most domestic water supplies in the United Kingdom are basically good brewing waters. The only problem waters are those which contain excessive amounts of chalk and this state is rarely serious. From experience the majority of people know

Treatment for Five Gallons (25 Litres) of Water

Type of Beer	Chalky Water	Non Chalky Water
Lager	1	—
Light Ale, Bitter, Pale Ale, Strong Ale, Barley Wine	1, 2	2
Brown Ale, Winter Ale, Mild Ale, Sweet Stout	1,3	3
Irish Stout	—	4

1. Add one teaspoonful of Flaked Calcium Chloride or Lactic Acid Solution.   or:
   Boil water for a quarter of an hour and rack off the soft water for use when cool.
2. Add one teaspoonful of Gypsum (Calcium Sulphate) and half a teaspoonful of Epsom Salts (Magnesium Sulphate).
3. Add half a teaspoonful of Common Salt (Sodium Chloride).
4. Add one teaspoonful of chalk (Calcium Carbonate).

N.B. One level teaspoonful = 5 ml.

whether water is hard or soft. If you reckon your water is hard then assume it contains chalk. Any doubt about it can easily be solved. Simply boil one gallon of water for a quarter of an hour and let it cool. Any chalk present will form a film or deposit on the boiler bottom. So now we have two categories for our water treatment: those with chalk and those without it.

Most home brew shops also stock proprietary ready made water treatments for the different types of beer which are perfectly satisfactory and an acceptable alternative to making your own as suggested above.

Yeast

Yeast converts the sugary wort into an alcoholic solution by the process called fermentation, and in doing so gives off copious amounts of carbon dioxide gas. In the brewery, it is the behaviour of the yeast that causes concern; in the pub it's the CO_2 gas! Yeast is a very unstable substance and needs careful attention in its natural wet state. Home brew yeasts are usually dried to give them better keeping qualities.

Fresh yeast from the brewery is best if you can get it. Understandably, not all breweries are willing to supply a sample although some are disappointed when you only want a cupful and not two or three cartloads of the liquid balm. We only need a small cupful to start off one of our brews. So long as it is sound, the yeast from one brew can be used to start the next one. Yeast reproduces about six times its volume during one fermentation so there is usually plenty to spare.

My second choice for a source of good yeast is from the beer itself. All naturally conditioned *real ales* contain yeast. One of the skills of the brewer and publican is to ensure the beer served to you contains only minute amounts. So don't go into your pub and ask for a 'cloudy pint of your best bitter with plenty of muck floating about in it please'—you might not appreciate your barman's sense of humour as he ceremoniously pours the treasured yeast brew over your head.

Seriously, half a pint of yeasty beer is what you want. Yeast sediment from a quickly consumed cask can provide a satisfactory medium for starting a batch of home brew. It is best to come to some arrangement with your landlord so he can take a sample at his convenience and not when the bar is busy. Keg beers cannot be used because the amount of yeast collected is insufficient to ensure a healthy fermentation.

Home Brewing Beer Yeasts

These yeasts are usually dried and are sold in sachets or tubs containing the coarse, light stone coloured granules. Yeast will only keep for about a week in the wet state. When dried, however, it can last for years and sounds the ideal arrangement for home brewing. Unfortunately, because yeast is a living thing, it suffers somewhat in processing. I don't suppose we would take kindly to dehydration or freeze drying either, but anyway, what comes out isn't as good as what went in. Dried yeasts need rehydrating in 2/3 cups of lukewarm water. Cover and leave for 15 minutes, then stir, before pitching the yeast in the wort. For those of us who do not live near a brewery, and have not mastered the skill of starting with half a pint of yeasty beer from the pub and ending up home with the same quantity, these dried yeasts are acceptable alternatives. I would recommend two sachets of good Brewing Yeast plus a dose of YEAST ENERGISER for a typical five gallon brew. Although slow, the fermentation with dried yeasts is usually very persistent and continues past the normal stopping point at the 'quarter gravity' figure. This continuing action results in a more alcoholic, less sweet and thinner bodied brew. Certain recipes call for the use of home brew beer yeast and these characteristics are catered for. However if you can only get home brew beer yeasts instead of the recommended commercial 'Brewer's Yeast' the flavour balance can be acceptably restored by adding five saccharin tablets. These tablets are in addition to any listed in the recipe. Barley Wine recipes are not subjected to these additions, however.

OTHER BREWING AIDS

Experience through the ages has shown the natural processes of brewing can be made more efficient and speeded up in some cases by the inclusion of other substances, for example, the mineral salts discussed above for water treatment. These additions are now accepted as part of the technique for traditional brewing. Besides these water treatment minerals, we have the following aids:

Isinglass

Isinglass has been used for centuries in beer to assist the clarification process in the cask. In the dry state it has a fine white fluffy texture and when prepared for brewing by dissolving in acid it forms a thick viscous liquid like wallpaper paste. Actually, isinglass is the shredded stomach of the sturgeon fish and I often muse on what else was tried for clearing beer before this was found to be successful. Next time you find 'floaters' in your beer make sure they are not swimming first. Nine times out of ten the minute whitish 'breadcrumbs' sometimes found in glasses of real ale are only these isinglass finings—which are perfectly natural and safe. Just clench your teeth and strain it out. Isinglass tends to be a bit unstable for home brewing unless the temperature can be maintained below 18°C.

Gelatine

Gelatine is the home brewer's answer to the instability of isinglass. One sachet of Davis Gelatine made up to a solution with warm water and added to beer will clear a full batch starbright within hours. After learning that isinglass is processed fish stomach it is probably no shock to learn that gelatine is produced from calves' heels. But think, now you can boast about your beers having a real kick in them! Packets of Davis Gelatine contain five half ounce (15 gm.) sachets and being readily available in most grocery shops it is another handy item to slip on to the household shopping budget.

Irish Moss

Outside the Emerald Isle, no one would really expect Irish Moss to be a type of lichen. Quite logically Irish Moss is seaweed. Commonly referred to as Copper finings, the small pieces of dried dark green seaweed are added to the boiling wort in the copper, the object being to hasten the 'hot break'; the stage when you have successfully 'coagulated your proteins' so they will drop out of solution and leave the murky wort clear. Incidentally, the dark green pieces of Irish Moss can be purchased as a fine white powder, which just about sums up this strange additive.

Chempro SDP

A quick acting combination cleanser/steriliser used by commercial breweries and now available to the home brew trade. The white powder is made up to varying strengths depending on the task. Follow the comprehensive instructions on the packet. It should never be added to beer.

Sodium Metabisulphite

Sulphur dioxide, the gas liberated from burning sulphur, has been used for centuries to purify wooden casks for beer and wine. Please take my word for it that burning sulphur kills all known germs. Once I tried to cure some wild hops by setting alight some sulphur in the dustbin containing them. My colleague decided to check progress and lifted the lid, only to be engulfed in billowing clouds of choking gas. We had to abandon the house for three hours to let the fumes disperse!

The safer, modern approach is to wash the equipment in a solution of sodium or potassium metabisulphite. A 10% strength (2 ozs. in 1 pint, 100 gm. in 1 litre) contained in an empty washing-up liquid dispenser makes a handy 'stock solution'. A two second burst into another pint of water makes a normal sterilising strength ideal for purifying bottles, casks, siphon tubes and other brewing equipment. Unlike the Chempro heavy duty cleaner and steriliser, the wet dregs of metabisulphite solution retained by the drained equipment does not require further rinsing with water to remove traces since it is harmless in low concentrations. Indeed SO_2 is the only permitted preservative allowed in commercial beer. A few drops of neat stock solution keeps beer bottles and casks sweet when empty. Do not use it in pressure barrels, as it will corrode any metal fittings in the cap, leading to unsafe and ineffective valves.

EQUIPMENT REQUIRED

Do not get carried away in your enthusiasm to brew some of these delicious beers and spend a fortune on home brew equipment. Using normal kitchen equipment and utensils it is possible to brew and handle 25 litres of beer for less than the price of a pint. Saucepans can be used to boil up the malt extract, hops and any sugar that is needed. An empty semi-rigid polythene cube with tap, contained in a cardboard box, will handle the rest of the processes. These containers (polypins, cubitainers) used to be very cheaply obtainable from off-licences and restaurants, but are now uncommon except from a few specialist suppliers. They proved very useful for resting the beer before kegging or bottling, and could be fitted with an airlock to protect the beer.

Although the technique works very well indeed, it is only suitable for the recipes based on malt extract and even with these beers you will probably want more finesse and want to consider the following equipment.

Bruheat Boiler

The Ritchie Products (Burton-on-Trent) Bruheat Boiler is a custom built boiler for home brewing. Basically, it is a 25 litre polypropylene bucket and lid, which has a kettle type of heating element fitted in the side walls near the bottom. The element is controlled by a very sensitive thermostat and is capable of automatically keeping the temperature of the liquid or mash inside to within a few degrees of a selected setting. Since the thermostat can be set between 10°C and 100°C it successfully copes with all the brewing processes of mashing, boiling and fermenting. A similar and equally efficient boiler is marketed by Thorne Electrim. Such a boiler costs about the equivalent of forty pints of beer at pub prices and is a most welcome birthday gift from your family! Alternatively there are many boilers or large dixies, with or without heating elements, that will do the job adequately.

Fermenting Vessel

Special white plastic fermenting bins are available in home brew shops and in large chain stores. One with a capacity of around 25 litres will cope with all recipes in this book. Ensure that it is supplied with a lid.

Hydrometer and Jar

A brewing hydrometer is a graduated float used for measuring the amount of sugar in a solution. Various facts and figures can be determined from its readings from alcohol potential, the amount actually produced, the efficiency and progress of the fermentation.

Bottles

Only use genuine sound returnable glass beer bottles for your brews. Considerable gas pressure is built up inside the bottle due to secondary fermentation set in motion to give the beer sparkle. Lemonade bottles and the like, although they contain pressurised liquids, generally are not designed to withstand beer pressures. These days, most beer bottles are sealed with disposable metal crown caps. Rebottling with home brew will require replacement seals. Crown caps and plastic reseals are readily available. A special inexpensive capping tool is needed to fit crown caps. (see photographs). Brown PET plastic bottles are also satisfactory.

Barrels

Currently in the U.K. there are about a dozen plastic pressure

24

barrels for bulk storage of home brew and all market CO_2 gas injection units for dispensing the beer under sterile pressure for those who prefer their beer served this way. All the ones featured have proven reliability by home brewers and can be recommended.

These are main items of expenditure which are included in the summary list below with other odds and ends and kitchen utensils needed to get one started on a five gallon malt extract brew.

Recommended Basic Equipment

Bruheat or Electrim Boiler or Large Boiler or Dixie.
6 gallon (25 litre) plastic fermenting bin with lid.
Hydrometer and jar.
Kitchen scales.
Large sieve.
Large saucepan.
Small funnel.
Kitchen spoons.
Siphon tubing.
Bottle brush.
5 gallon (25 litre) 'worth' of beer bottles or
Large pressure barrel.
Thermometer (0–100°C).
5–one gallon jars or a five gallon fermenter with airlock.

To this list I would add a grain bag which is really essential for mashing recipes.

Grain Bag

Mashed grains can be awkward to handle, but contained in the grain bag as shown are very easy to manage.

Mashing grain bags and insert bags for the Bruheat boiler can be purchased in better home brew shops and are really essential for handling the mashed grain.

To make one, buy your wife/girlfriend a box of chocolates and ask her to do it for you! The bag should have a capacity of about 4 gallons (18 litres). Its cross section can either be square or round depending on what shape the mash tun is. For efficient extraction, the side walls need to be made from some strong, fairly impervious material, e.g. canvas, which can be used for the straps as well. Plastic diamond mesh (⅛ in. : 3 mm.) as sold in gardening shops makes an ideal sieve for the bottom. Note that the grain bag holds over 20 lbs. (9 kg.) weight of hot wet grain and must be very well constructed.

CHAPTER 3

ENJOYING YOUR BREWING

LETS get going and try your hand at brewing a batch of draught Fullers Extra Special Bitter and then some bottled Guinness Extra Stout.

I have chosen these beers which cover both malt extract and malted barley methods of brewing. These are beginners examples and will contain the fullest production details and explanations of why we are carrying out the various stages and what we hope to achieve. The thought behind these processes must be remembered for the main recipe section of the book which will only lay down the basic instructions for making particular beers.

FULLERS E.S.B.

Fullers E.S.B. is one of the strongest draught beers in the country and has a full malty flavour with a beautiful hop flavour rather than bitterness rounded off by just the right degree of sweetness.

Our home brew version will be based on malt extract syrup and is an excellent example of how commercial type beer can be produced by simple procedures.

4½ gallons	Alcohol 5·5%	22.5 litres
4 lb.	Edme D.M.S. Malt Extract	2000 gm.
5 oz.	Crushed Crystal Malt	150 gm.
2 lb.	Soft Brown Sugar	1000 gm.
(2½+¼+¼) oz.	Goldings Hops	(75+10+10) gm.
½ oz.	Home Brew Beer Yeast	15 gm.
5	Saccharin tablets	5
1 tsp.	Irish Moss	5 ml.
1 tsp.	Gypsum	5 ml.
½ oz.	Gelatine	15 gm.
1 oz.	White sugar	30 gm.

Method:

Boiling

Add the malt extract, crystal malt, gypsum and Irish moss to

26

3 gallons (15 litres) of hot water in the boiler or large dixie. Stir thoroughly to dissolve the malt extract completely before applying more heat. The first quota (2½ oz./75 gm.) of hops can now be mixed in and the heat applied. Boil for 35 minutes. The first 10 minutes of the boil will see the wort kick and froth up with alarming rapidity—so keep a watchful eye on progress. At the end of the boiling period, switch off the heat, leave the wort for a minute or so and then stir in the second quota of Goldings (¼ oz./10 gm).

Sterilise Equipment

Meanwhile clean and sterilise the intended fermenting bin with Chempro powder used as directed on the instructions.

Strain Off

Using a large sieve or the grain bag, strain the wort through the mesh into the fermenting bin. Wash out the remaining extract from the spent hops with a kettleful of hot water. The used hops can be discarded.

Add Sugar

Dissolve the brown sugar and saccharins in some hot water and add this to the fermenting bin as well. Top up the wort to the 4½ gallon mark with cold water.

Check Specific Gravity

When the wort temperature cools to ambient check the specific gravity with a hydrometer. The instrument is simply floated in the wort and the reading is taken at the liquid level. Hydrometers often have three scales, but the one we are interested in is marked with figures 0.990 to around 1.120 and denotes gravity. By some magic property, hydrometers always seem to stop spinning in the wort so that the scale you want to read faces the other way! Disregard the other scales on the instrument as these are used for winemaking; the information could confuse your thoughts in brewing. The specific gravity reading should be within a degree or two of 1047. It is a good idea to start a recipe book and note all this process data as it can be invaluable for making any minor alterations to the recipe which you feel are necessary to 'tone-in' the brewing equipment and ingredients nearer your interpretation of the original brew.

Primary Fermentation

Having noted the original gravity, the cooled wort is ready

to receive the yeast. One sachet of dried Home Brewing Beer yeast can be rehydrated and pitched in. In the initial stages, yeast requires plenty of oxygen from the air to assist the reproduction process. Using a sterilised plastic brewing 'paddle' or spoon, aeration is best achieved by stirring from the bottom and lifting the wort and yeast to the surface. Replace the lid on the fermenting bin and store the beer in a reasonably warm place with the minimum of temperature fluctuations. A constant temperature of 18°C is ideal. Too low, the fermentation will be slow and the beer will develop yeast taints; too high, the brew may fall foul of sickly acid flavours.

Within a day the surface of the brew should be covered with a light fluffy meringue like topping of yeast. The crop will build up and sometimes form long protruding tentacles—quite a frightening sight the first time you see it. Also this initial yeast crop will purge the beer of unwanted hop fractions and protein debris. The dirty, brownish grey scum formed is best skimmed off the clean yeast.

Beneath the crop the beer will appear to 'simmer' through the vigorous liberation of carbon dioxide gas and the suspended yeast will give it a milky appearance. Certain strains of yeast tend to drop out of solution easily or congregate at the surface. These yeasts need stirring back in or rousing daily to ensure the fermentation progresses at a reasonable rate. Progress is easily checked by taking the hydrometer readings. Over the next two or three days readings should progressively fall to around 10 (S.G. 1010).

As fermentation abates the amount of carbon dioxide gas given off also decreases. Thus there is less gas to give the yeast buoyancy so the beer under the yeast pancake will start to clear. The primary fermentation has now produced the alcohol and the beer is ready for the next stage.

Secondary Fermentation

The object of this intermediate stage of secondary fermentation is to remove the excess yeast and prepare the brew for its final casking.

The beer has got to be transferred to another vessel or vessels fitted with airlocks. Five individual one gallon jars can be used, or a five gallon fermenter with airlock. Clean and sterilise the five gallon fermenter and add one teaspoonful (5 ml.) of sugar.

28

Replace lid.

Gelatine Finings

Sprinkle the contents of one sachet of Davis Gelatine into a small saucepanful of cold water. Let it stand for a few minutes to absorb and then apply gentle heat whilst stirring continuously. Completely dissolve the gelatine granules before the mixture boils. Add these finings to the empty fermenter.

Prepare for Syphoning

Position the bin full of beer on a table or shelf to give about one metre of head pressure above the fermenter. Place the hook end of the syphon tube in the beer and suck the other end of the tube to fill it with beer. Press this end to seal it and place it through the top of the fermenter. Release the pressure and allow the beer to flow. Keep the outlet end below the surface of the beer to minimise aeration. Transfer all the beer except the sediment. Stir the contents of the fermenter thoroughly, to disperse the gelatine finings. Replace the lid, or cap, and transfer the container to a cool place, around 13°C, but not lower than 7°C.

If you have a polypin cube or a five-gallon 'Drafty' the beer can be stored in this, and the tap in the filler cap can be prised out and the hole left is just the right size bore to fit a standard airlock bung. Alternatively, a bottle airlock system can be used as shown in the diagram on page 65. Actually since this particular brew will not completely fill the cube, the latter method is best. Before fitting the airlock add the final quota of hops. Dry hopping restores the hop aroma.

Now safe and sterile away from contact with air, the beer can be left indefinitely like this. In fact, three weeks is preferable, although since this is a beginners exercise a week is adequate. I cannot have you dying of thirst while attempting your first brew up!

Fullers E.S.B.

The crystal clear brew can be racked into another container, and back into the washed polypin if you have one, taking care to leave the hops and sediment behind. Add the white sugar direct.

Stillage

The ideal place to keep the beer is within arm's reach of your favourite chair. Feet up, telly on, a full cask of beer and what

29

more do you need? I keep protesting that the arrangement looks very attractive with the simulated wood effect cardboard casing, but mine always gets relegated to the cupboard under

the stairs. I console myself that the cooler environment there is better for conditioning the beer.

Check Pressure Daily

Polythene cubes or polypins are sealed containers and do not have an automatic safety valve to vent excess pressure. In the above procedure I have endeavoured to ensure that there is only sufficient unfermented sugar in the beer just to condition it. The ullage space created by the under filled capacity will cope with the conditioning pressure. Extra hot days, though, may cause the cube to balloon slightly. Check the arrangement DAILY and vent any excessive pressure by drawing off a pint. I was going to say . . . and drink the beer, but it should not take long for you to realise these brewer's perks!

Keep Air Out

My early comments about beer in contact with air apply to

drawing off pints. Initially the conditioning pressure will ensure air is kept out, but when the cube is half empty or when a number of pints are drawn off in quick succession, air could bubble in. On these occasions create and maintain external pressure by sliding and pressing down the palm of your hand on the top of the cube before opening the tap. Pressure barrels are much more reliable; they keep your beer under pressure and vent surplus gas automatically, and are far less likely to split or leak—always a danger with polypins, which do not normally contain liquid under pressure.

Pressure Barrels

This gorgeous bitter has been designed to be dispensed as 'real ale' without external CO_2 pressure. But Fullers E.S.B. is often served with top pressure and if you prefer your beer this way then fit a CO_2 injector unit to the pressure barrel cap.

The filling technique is similar to the method described above. Clear beer is siphoned from the 'secondary' fermenter into the sterilised barrel and filled to leave a quart of ullage

space. Add the white sugar. Prepare the gas injector unit. Close the control valve. Fit a new CO_2 cartridge and screw in the holder to puncture it. Screw the filler cap *loosely* on the barrel thread. Open the control valve for a second or two to let a burst of CO_2 gas into the ullage space. This action will purge out any air present. Screw the filler cap on tight and inject another burst of gas. This time the excess pressure will vent from the safety valve almost immediately. The beer is now under pressure and can be drawn off.

Other CO_2 injector units regulate the pressure automatically or just inject CO_2 to push the beer out of the barrel. The latter type usually have a handle which acts as the control valve to let the gas in. Use these devices strictly as directed on the instructions.

TRY SOME GUINNESS EXTRA STOUT

The final part of your brewing apprenticeship is to try your hand at brewing five gallons of Guinness which, by my reckoning, is the best beer in the world.

As with the majority of beers in this book, Guinness is based on malted barley grains and this recipe demonstrates how to brew a typical 'grain' beer. Differences in the common mashing methods will be highlighted.

Method

5 gallons	Original Gravity 1045	25 litres
7 lb.	Crushed pale malt	3500 gm.
2 lb.	Flaked barley	1000 gm.
1 lb.	Crushed roast barley	500 gm.
1 oz.	Bullion hops	30 gm.
3 oz.	Northern brewer hops	100 gm.
	Yeast from Whitebread White Shield, or any other of the many bottle-conditioned beers now on sale—eg, Shepherd Neame's Spitfire, Nethergate's Old Growler, the supermarket Sainsbury's own brand Bottle Conditioned Ale	
	Temporary hard water (containing chalk)	

Brewing this stout takes some planning because you will be using the yeast from a bottle of Whitbread White Shield. Four or five days before the main brewing session take a trip down to your neglected 'local' and purchase a pint bottle of White Shield. Try without exhausting your landlord's patience too much to select a bottle with a good ring of yeast clinging to the bottom. Ideally the bottles should be inspected under a strong light to assess the amount of yeast deposit. If there is any doubt, buy two or three pints and drink the surplus beer. Although one bottle is usually sufficient to provide a good working starter in a few days, the 'tops' of the other pints do give an excuse to savour the impressively smooth, full bodied, dry bitter taste pleasantly peculiar to White Shield.

The yeast lifted from a bottle of Guinness was the best I have come across for home brewing top fermented English beers, but since April 1993 all Guinness supplied in mainland Britain has been pasteurised.

Making a Yeast Starter

It is worth taking extra care with the cultivation of a good yeast sample. Yeast performance and characteristics vary with the gravity and nutrient properties of the wort and can be ruined by an alien environment. Bearing this in mind I like to make up my starter to emulate a Guinness wort. A three quarter pint (400 ml.) starter comprising of the bottom third of the White Shield bottle topped up with a mixture of one tablespoonful (50 gm.) of malt extract syrup in water should do the trick.

The day before brewing, the yeast in the starter bottle should be working vigorously. Do not start the brewing session unless you are confident the yeast is strong enough to be pitched in to finish the job.

Methods of Mashing

There are two distinct techniques for mashing at home and I will describe examples for each method. Which one you choose depends largely on how much you can afford. The more you spend, the less effort you employ!

Method 1—Dixie or Large Boiling Pan

As many home brewers already possess a boiler of some sort for their beermaking it is likely that this piece of essential equipment will double up as a mash tun as well. To cater for the largest brews requiring up to 10 lb. of dry grain, the boiler, dixie or large boiling pan used should not be smaller than a 4½ gallon capacity

The dry grains and cereals need to be mixed with hot water to form a smooth 'porridge' To achieve the correct mix of grist (includes all crushed malt grains, roast malts, flaked and flavoured cereals) to water use the following ratios

For Mashing

Mix 1 lb. of grist with 2½–3 pints of water
or 1 kg. of grist with 3.25–3.75 litres of water.

For our Guinness brew the grist totals 7 lb. of malt, 2 lb. of barley and 1 lb of roast barley giving 10 lb. of grain. From the above guidelines, ideally, 30 pints of water are required for mashing, although 25 pints can be tolerated with limited mashing capacity.

Pour the water and water treatment salts into the pan. Apply heat and raise the temperature up to 60°C. Gradually stir in the dry grist to form a smooth mixture. Keep stirring and slowly raise the temperature of the mix up to 67°C. Switch off the heat and let the mash stand for 1½ hours. It will be necessary to reheat the mash back to the temperature 65°–67°C a couple of times as it cools. When applying heat during any mashing technique, continual stirring is essential to prevent hot spots prematurely killing off the enzymes which do the starch conversion.

Method 2—Bruheat Boiler

As in method 1, use thirty pints of water and follow the above procedure for the initial mixing and raising up to 67°C. Afterwards set the dial setting to keep the mash temperature between 62–66°C. The selection is made by finding the dial setting which makes the thermostat click on and off. From then the process needs no further attention except for an occasional stir.

Method 3—Floating Mash Tun

Brewers with large (10 gallon/50 litre) boilers can often enjoy the convenience of the floating mash tun system. Half fill the boiler and raise the water temperature to 75°C. Contain the dry grist in a grain bag lining a large bucket fitted with a tap and lid. Mix the grain with the boiler water to form a thick mix. The temperature of the resultant mix should be around 66°C. Replace the bucket lid and float the mash tun in the remaining boiler water for 1½ hours to complete the

METHODS OF MASHING

① USING BOILING PAN OR DIXIE

MIX THE CRUSHED MALT
GRAINS WITH HOT WATER
IN A BOILING PAN AND
KEEP TEMPERATURE AS
CLOSE TO 66°C (150°F)
FOR 1½ HOURS

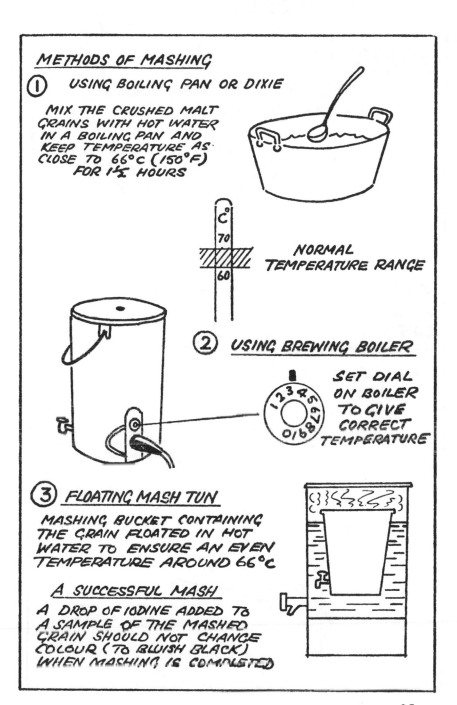

NORMAL
TEMPERATURE RANGE

② USING BREWING BOILER

SET DIAL
ON BOILER
TO GIVE
CORRECT
TEMPERATURE

③ FLOATING MASH TUN

MASHING BUCKET CONTAINING
THE GRAIN FLOATED IN HOT
WATER TO ENSURE AN EVEN
TEMPERATURE AROUND 66°C

A SUCCESSFUL MASH

A DROP OF IODINE ADDED TO
A SAMPLE OF THE MASHED
GRAIN SHOULD NOT CHANGE
COLOUR (TO BLUISH BLACK)
WHEN MASHING IS COMPLETED

35

SPARGING

EXTRACTING THE GOODNESS FROM BARLEY MALT

GENTLY WASH THE GRAIN WITH HOT WATER

MASHED MALT HELD IN A GRAIN BAG SIEVE SUPPORTED IN A POLYTHENE BUCKET

BOILER

The main ingredients for brewing: Sterilisers for equipment, malts, hops, yeasts and additives.

Ritchie 'Bruheat' boiler, plus a range of ingredients.

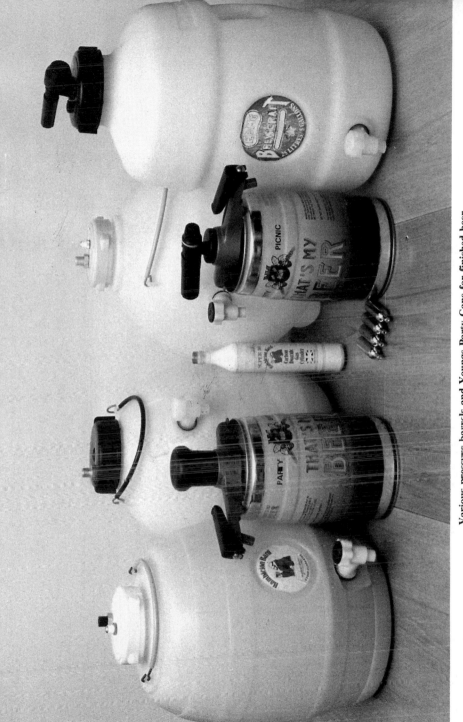

Various pressure barrels and Youngs Party Cans for finished beer, gas bulbs, and a Hambleton Bard gas cylinder.

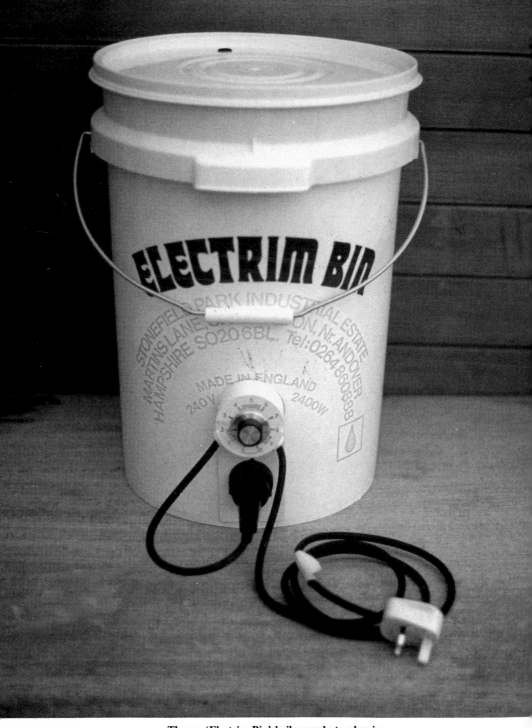

Thorne 'Electrim Bin' boiler ready to plug in.

Mashing and straining bags from Vina.

Equipment for brewing and fermenting.

Bottling equipment: Mallet and capper, two-handed capper, crown caps, plastic reseals, internal and external screw stoppers, standard and EZ-type bottles.

Beer, glorious beer!

mashing. After saccharification, the boiler water can be removed and used to rinse the extract from the mashed grain back into the boiler for the boil with the hops.

Sparging Your Wort!

It is worth starting home brewing just to have this exhilarating experience—What other hobby can offer such a wealth of verbal expressions? Telling people you have been sparging your wort initiates some incredible responses from blank disbelief to utter disgust!

Actually it's the retrieval of the rich malt sugars from the mashed grain. And it is a very necessary stage in our brewing.

Depending on the mashing method you adopted, the mashed grain may or may not be already contained in the grain bag. If it is not, as would be the case with the boiler methods, the hot grain must be transferred to the grain bag. First of all the bag must be supported or contained someway so that the wort can be run off into another rece.ver or direct into the boiler. Obviously the floating mash tun bucket satisfies this requirement already. I made a simple wort tray using a cut off section from a polythene cube for using after mashing in my Bruheat. Alternatively the bag can be supported in a bucket with a tap.

The rich wort will start draining off immediately but will be rather cloudy and hence it is best to collect the first jug or so and return it to the surface of the grain before letting the rest flow into the boiler. Let the grains drain naturally until reasonably dry then gently jug hot water (around 70°C) over the grain surface. Continue this sparging with more hot water until 4 gallons (20 litres) of wort are collected.

Boiling

Boil the wort with all the hops for one hour. Strain the wort off the hops into a fermenting bin and top up to the final quantity with cold water.

Brewing Efficiency

When cool the 5 gallons of wort should float a specific gravity between 1045 and 1053. In designing this recipe I purposely erred on the 'strong' side so a beginner to mashing could, even with an inefficient extraction, still brew a stout with the strength of Guinness. The high figure of 1053 is what a commercial brewery would be likely to achieve with so-phisticated plant.

Using my mashing methods, you should achieve an original gravity of 1045 quite easily.

Fermentation

Getting back to the brewing, the cooled wort is now ready to receive the yeast. Pitch in the starter bottle contents and aerate the wort for a minute or two. Replace the bin lid and ferment the wort in a warm place. After three or four days when the specific gravity has fallen to around 1012 rack the beer into a sterilised container fitted with an airlock. Let the stout stand in this vessel for another week to fall bright naturally.

Bottling

Collect 'five gallons worth' of beer bottles. Never use the fragile one-trip disposable bottles. Inspect them to ensure they are mechanically sound; no chips, cracks etc., and give them a thorough cleaning using Chempro powder. Afterwards give the bottles a good rinse out with cold water. Alternatively, a bit of hard work with hot water and a bottle brush will satisfy the cleaning requirements, although the bottles need sterilising to ensure purity.

Sterilising Bottles

Add a generous burst of 10% sodium metabisulphite solution to a pint of hot water and funnel the mix from one bottle to another. Drain thoroughly, but do not bother to rinse.

Priming

The stout at this stage retains very little carbon dioxide gas and is flat. To promote condition and more gas in the bottle the fermentation process must be rekindled. Line up the bottles and funnel into each one a dose of white sugar at the rate of half a level teaspoonful per pint of capacity (5 ml. per litre). Alternatively, stir into the bulk beer, 2½ oz. (75 g.) of sugar dissolved in a little hot water.

Filling

Position the container of stout on a table or shelf and line up the bottles on the floor below. Useful accessories are an empty beer glass and a mopping up cloth. The glass to have crafty 'sippers' to check that it is all right (very essential) and the cloth to soak up any spillages that might and usually do occur.

Siphon the beer into the bottles. Keep the end of the tube near the bottle bottom to avoid frothing. It is essential that the bottles are not completely filled. Leave an airspace; a minimum of ¾ in. per pint or 40 mm. per litre bottle. The airspace above the beer acts as a safety reservoir to contain the excess gas given off by the bottle fermentation.

Fit the bottle seals as appropriate.

Maturation

Guinness requires seven to ten day maturation in the bottle stored in a reasonably warm place, then transfer the bottles to a cool storage place. Start supping the ale after this time to check its condition. Like the real thing, our stout is best consumed within a month which is rarely a problem for thirsty home brewers.

Draught Guinness

Draught Guinness is one of few examples where modern technology has benefitted a beer from the drinkers point of view. In a keg process, Guinness is injected mainly with nitrogen gas instead of the usual carbon dioxide. Nitrogen promotes a much smoother flavour and promotes a fine creamy head. I have injected my home brew version with nitrogen gas with a remarkable degree of success, but the system is out of the scope of most home brewers. Using a measure of heading liquid or powder and dispensing the stout under pressure from a barrel is an acceptable compromise. Draught Guinness is approximately 80% of strength of the bottled version with original gravity around 1038. Use the same ratio of ingredients, but cut down by one fifth for the draught version. Alternatively dilute the five gallon brew up to six and a quarter gallons, but somehow I just cannot bring myself to do this. Adding water to this excellent ale seems sacrilege.

CHAPTER 4

BREWING YOUR FAVOURITE BEERS

YOU are now ready to tackle brewing any of the hundred or so beers in the main recipe section. Only the basic facts about the brewing ingredients and method required will be given.

There are four columns of information regarding the ingredients. The main list is the ingredients itself and is flanked by both imperial and metric quantities. Do not however cross reference the two weight systems as the final volumes of beer will not be the same. i.e. 5 gallons is not equivalent to 25 litres and the ingredients list reflects this difference.

The first column on the left hand side gives a STAGE number reference for each ingredient. This number refers to the BREWING STAGE at which this particular ingredient is used. Certain ingredients have the weight subdivided as in the Arkell Brown Jack recipe (see Page 43) where the roast barley is listed as $(2\frac{1}{2}+\frac{1}{2})$ oz. with corresponding STAGE references of 1 and 2. This means that $2\frac{1}{2}$ oz. are used in brewing Stage 1 and $\frac{1}{2}$ oz. is used later in Stage 2.

Another point to clarify on the ingredients list is regarding the concentrated hop extracts. Sometimes these are sold in tubs marked 'Sufficient for 4 gallons'. In these instances take this to mean the contents are equivalent to 4 oz. of hops and apportion them accordingly.

Each recipe recommends using water to suit the type of beer being brewed. The recommended water treatments (if needed) are listed on Page 19. Also most recipes call for the use of Irish Moss, which, if no instructions are given, should be added during the last ten minutes of the boiling stage. Omitting the water treatment, Irish Moss and Gelatine finings will not stop you brewing a good beer but may prevent you ending up with an excellent one true to type as I intended.

To simplify the brewing stages I have only described the mashing method applicable to the brewing boiler techniques (Methods 1 and 2). The alternative mashing equipment requires a modified approach as suggested in the trial stout recipe. Actually, it is easier to follow the instructions rather than read about them—so get started with your brewing now.

BOTTLED BEERS

CHAPTER 5

CARLSBERG–TETLEY
SKOL LAGER

A VERY popular lager and one of the major selling brands. Lightly flavoured with a refreshing bite.

Stage	5 gallons	Original gravity 1034	25 litres
1	3 gallons	Water for 'lager' brewing	15 litres
1	5 lb.	Crushed lager malt	2500 gm.
1	3 oz.	Crushed wheat malt	100 gm.
1	12 oz.	Flaked maize	400 gm.
3	8 oz.	Brewing sugar	250 gm.
3	1½ oz.	Hallertau hops	50 gm.
3	1 oz.	Goldings hops	30 gm.
3	1 tsp.	Irish moss	5 ml.
5	2 oz.	Lager yeast	60 gm.
5	½ oz.	Gelatine	15 gm.
6	½ tsp/pint	White sugar	5 ml./litre

Brewing Stages

1. Raise the temperature of the water up to 40°C and stir in the crushed malt and flaked maize. Stirring continuously, raise the mash temperature up to 55°C. Let it stand for half an hour and then raise the temperature again up to 66°C. Leave for 1½ hours, occasionally returning the temperature back to this value.

2. Contain the mashed grain in a large grain bag to retrieve the sweet wort. Using slightly hotter water than the mash, rinse the grains to collect 4 gallons (20 litres) of extract.

3. Boil the extract with the hops for 1½ hours. Dissolve the main batch of sugar in a little hot water and add this during the boil. Also pitch in the Irish Moss as directed on the instructions.

4. Switch off the heat. Strain off the clear wort into a fermenting bin and top up to the final quantity with cold water.

5. When cool to room temperature add the yeast. Ferment in a cool place (10°C) until the specific gravity falls to 1010 and rack into gallon jars or a five gallon fermenter with airlock. Apportion gelatine finings before fitting airlocks.

6. Leave for 21 days before racking the beer from the sediment into primed beer bottles. Allow 30 days maturation before sampling. Serve chilled.

ARKELL Swindon

BROWN JACK BEST BROWN ALE

An excellent brown ale with a distinctive flavour of freshly roasted grain. The deep garnet colour topped with a fine white creamy head looks really impressive.

Stage	2 gallons	3.5% Alcohol	10 litres
1	2 lb.	Dark malt extract	1000 gm.
1, 2	(2½ + ½) oz.	Crushed roast barley	(75 + 15) gm.
1	12 oz.	Brown sugar	400 gm.
1	1 oz.	Fuggles hops	30 gm.
1	2 gallons	Water for 'brown ale' brewing	10 litres
2	2	Saccharin tablets	2
2	1 oz.	Home brew beer yeast	30 gm.
3	½ tsp./pint	White sugar	5 ml./litre

Brewing Stages

1. Boil the malt extract, first quota of roast barley and the hops in 2 gallons (10 litres) of water for 45 minutes. Carefully strain off the wort from the hops and malt grains into a fermenting bin. Rinse the spent grains and hops with 2 kettlefuls of hot water. Dissolve the brown sugar in hot water and add this to the bin. Top up to the final quantity with cold water.

2. When cool to room temperature pitch in the yeast, saccharin tablets and the rest of the roast barley. Ferment 4–5 days until the activity abates. Rack off into secondary fermentation vessels and keep under airlock protection for another 7 days.

3. Rack the beer off the sediment into primed beer bottles. Allow 10 days maturation before sampling.

BASS

CARLING BLACK LABEL

British brewed version of a well known Canadian brew and the strongest of the 'Big Six' breweries main line lagers.

Stage	5 gallons	Original gravity 1039	25 litres
1	4½ lbs.	Crushed lager malt	2250 gm.
1	3 gallons	Water for 'lager' brewing	15 litres
3	2 lb.	White sugar	1000 gm.
3	1 tsp.	Irish moss	5 ml.
3	3 oz.	Hallertau hops	100 gm.
5	2 oz.	Lager yeast	60 gm.
5	½ oz.	Gelatine	15 gm.
6	½ tsp./pint	Brown sugar	5 ml./litre

Brewing Stages

1. Raise the temperature of the water up to 45°C and stir in the crushed malt. Sitrring continuously raise the mash temperature up to 55°C. Let it stand for half an hour and then raise the temperature again up to 66°C. Leave for one hour occasionally returning the temperature back to this value.

2. Contain the mashed grain in a large grain bag to retrieve the sweet wort. Using slightly hotter water than the mash, rinse the grains to collect 4 gallons (20 litres) of extract.

3. Boil the extract with the hops for 1½ hours. Dissolve the sugar in a little water and add this during the boil. Also pitch in the Irish Moss as directed on the instructions.

4. Switch off the heat. Strain off the clear wort into a fermenting bin and top up to the final quantity with cold water.

5. When cool to room temperature add the yeast. Ferment in a cool place until the specific gravity falls to 1010 and rack into gallon jars or a secondary fermentation vessel, fitted with an airlock. Apportion Gelatine finings before fitting airlocks.

6. Leave for 21 days before racking the beer from the sediment into primed beer bottles. Allow 21 days maturation before sampling.

BASS

BASS OR TOBY LIGHT ALE

Satisfying, appetising beery bouquet. Malty and hoppy in flavour bordering on pale ale characteristics.

Toby Jugs

The Toby Jug was inspired by Toby Fillpot, the nickname for Henry Elwes the great glutton and star drunkard of the 18th century, who it is said consumed 20,000 gallons of ale in his lifetime.

Stage	5 gallons	Original gravity 1035	25 litres
1	4¾ lb.	Crushed pale malt	2400 gm.
1	2½ gallons	Water for 'pale ale' brewing	12 litres
3	1 tsp.	Irish moss	5 ml.
3	12 oz.	Malt extract syrup	400 gm.
3	8 oz.	Soft brown sugar	250 gm.
3	2 oz.	Fuggles hops	60 gm.
3	1½ oz.	Bramling Cross hops	45 gm.
5	2 oz.	Brewers yeast	60 gm.
5	½ oz.	Gelatine	15 gm.
6	½ tsp./pint	White sugar	5 ml./litre

Brewing Stages

1. Raise the temperature of the water up to 60°C and stir in the crushed malt. Stirring continuously, raise the mash temperature up to 66°C. Leave for 1½ hours occasionally returning the temperature back to this value.
2. Contain the mashed grain in a large grain bag to retrieve the sweet wort. Using slightly hotter water than the mash, rinse the grains to collect 4 gallons (20 litres) of extract.
3. Boil the extract with the hops for 1½ hours. Dissolve the malt extract and the main batch of sugar in a little hot water and add this during the boil. Also pitch in the Irish Moss as directed on the instructions.
4. Switch off the heat, strain off the clear wort into a fermenting bin and top up to the final quantity with cold water.
5. When cool to room temperature add the yeast. Ferment 4–5 days until the specific gravity falls to 1010 and rack into gallon jars or a five gallon fermenter with airlock. Apportion Gelatine finings before fitting airlocks.
6. Leave for 7 days before racking the beer from the sediment into primed beer bottles. Allow 10 days maturation before sampling.

BASS Birmingham

WORTHINGTON WHITE SHIELD

One of the few naturally conditioned bottled beers brewed in the United Kingdom and truly 'an esteemed ale of fine flavour and unblemished tradition'.

Stage	4 gallons	Original gravity 1052	20 litres
1	6½ lb.	Crushed pale malt	3250 gm.
1	6 oz.	Crushed crystal malt	200 gm.
1	3 gallons	Water for 'pale ale' brewing	15 litres
3	1 tsp.	Irish moss	5 ml.
3	1 lb.	Brewing sugar	500 gm.
3	2 oz.	Fuggles hops	60 gm.
3, 4, 5	(1 + ½ + ¼) oz.	Goldings hops	(30 + 15 + 10) gm.
5	½ oz.	Gelatine	15 gm.
5		Yeast starter from Worthington White Shield bottle	
6	½ tsp./pint	White sugar	5 ml./litre

Brewing Stages

1. Raise the temperature of the water up to 60°C and stir in the crushed malts. Stirring continuously raise the mash temperature up to 66°C. Leave for 1½ hours occasionally returning the temperature back to this value.

2. Contain the mashed grain in a large grain bag to retrieve the sweet wort. Using slightly hotter water than the mash, rinse the grains to collect 4 gallons (20 litres) of extract.

3. Boil the extract with the Fuggles hops and the first quota of Goldings hops for 1½ hours. Dissolve the main batch of sugar in a little hot water and add this during the boil. Also pitch in the Irish Moss as directed on the instructions.

4. Switch off the heat, stir in the second batch of Goldings and allow them to soak for 15 minutes. Strain off the clear wort into a fermenting bin and top up to the final quantity with cold water.

5. When cool to room temperature add the yeast. Ferment 4–5 days until the specific gravity falls to 1012 and rack into gallon jars or a secondary fermentation vessel, fitted with an airlock. Apportion Gelatine finings and the rest of the dry hops before fitting airlocks.

6. Leave for 5 days before racking the beer from the sediment into primed beer bottles. Allow 21 days conditioning before sampling.

CARLSBERG Northampton

SPECIAL BREW LAGER

A very strong beautifully balanced beer; the lager equivalent of our barley wines. Backed by the best of Danish brewing experience and brewed at the Carlsberg Brewery in Northampton, this lager is really a 'special brew'.

Stage	3 gallons	Original gravity 1080	15 litres
1	5¾ lb.	Crushed lager malt	2900 gm.
1	1½ lb.	Flaked maize	750 gm.
1	3 gallons	Water for 'lager' brewing	15 litres
3	1 tsp.	Irish moss	5 ml.
3	1½ lb.	Golden syrup	750 gm.
3, 4	(2½ + ½) oz.	Hallertau hops	(75 + 15) gm.
5	1 oz.	Lager yeast	30 gm.
5	½ oz.	Gelatine	15 gm.
6	½ tsp./pint	White sugar	5 ml./litre

Brewing Stages

1. Raise the temperature of the water up to 45°C and stir in the crushed malt and flakes. Stirring continuously raise the mash temperature up to 55°C. Let it stand for half an hour and then raise the temperature again up to 66°C. Leave for 1½ hours occasionally returning the temperature back to this value.
2. Contain the mashed grain in a large grain bag to retrieve the sweet wort. Using slightly hotter water than the mash, rinse the grains to collect 3 gallons (15 litres) of extract.
3. Boil the extract with the hops for 1½ hours. Dissolve the syrup in a little hot water and add this during the boil. Also pitch in the Irish Moss as directed on the instructions.
4. Switch off the heat, stir in the second batch of hops and allow them to soak for 15 minutes. Strain off the clear wort into a fermenting bin and top up to the final quantity with cold water.
5. When cool to room temperature add the yeast. Ferment until the specific gravity falls to 1020 and rack into gallon jars. Apportion Gelatine finings and top up before fitting airlocks.
6. Leave for 30 days before racking the beer from the sediment into primed beer bottles. Allow 30 days conditioning before sampling. Chill before serving.

On top of the highly sophisticated brewing control pane at Carlsberg's Northampton Brewery is a glass case containing a Lager Beer Kit with a notice 'In an emergency break glass and use!'

COURAGE

IMPERIAL RUSSIAN STOUT

A beautifully smooth naturally conditioned dark barley wine originally brewed for the Tsarist Court where it found favour in the 18th century. The strongest beer regularly brewed in the United Kingdom.

Stage	2 gallons	Original gravity 1103	10 litres
1	6 lb.	Crushed pale malt	3000 gm.
1	½ lb.	Crushed crystal malt	250 gm.
1	¼ lb.	Crushed chocolate malt	125 gm.
1	¼ lb.	Crushed black malt	125 gm.
1	3 gallons	Water for 'barley wine' brewing	15 litres
3	1 lb.	Soft dark brown sugar	500 gm.
3	3 oz.	Fuggles hops	100 gm.
4	½ oz.	Wine yeast	15 gm.
6	½ tsp./pint	White sugar	5 ml./litre

Brewing Stages

1. Raise the temperature of the water up to 60°C and stir in the crushed malts. Stirring continuously, raise the mash temperature up to 66°C. Leave for 1½ hours occasionally returning the temperature back to this value.
2. Contain the mashed grain in a large grain bag to retrieve the sweet wort. Using slightly hotter water than the mash slowly and gently rinse the grains to collect 3½ gallons (16 litres) of extract.
3. Boil the extract with the hops and the sugar dissolved in a little water until the volume has been reduced to just over 2 gallons (10 litres). Strain off and divide equally in three gallon jars. Fit airlocks.
4. When cool add a wine yeast and ferment until the vigorous activity abates. Then siphon off into two one gallon jars, filling each to the base of the neck. Refit airlocks, and check regularly to ensure they don't dry out.
5. It will take months to complete the fermentation, after which the stout should be racked again taking with it a minute quantity of the yeast sediment.
6. Store for six months before bottling in primed beer bottles (preferably 'nips').
7. Mature for 18 months before sampling.

ELDRIDGE POPE Dorchester

KONIG PILSNER

Well established English brewed lager that has been around long before the current surge in popularity of continental styled beers.

Stage	5 gallons	Original gravity 1035	25 litres
1	5 lb.	Crushed lager malt	2500 gm.
1	1 lb.	Flaked rice	500 gm.
1	3 gallons	Water for 'lager' brewing	15 litres
3	8 oz.	Brewing sugar	250 gm.
3	1½ oz.	Hallertau hops	45 gm.
3	½ oz.	Goldings hops	15 gm.
3	1 tsp.	Irish moss	5 ml.
5	2 oz.	Lager yeast	60 gm.
5	½ oz.	Gelatine	15 gm.
6	½ tsp./pint	White sugar	5 ml./litre

Brewing Stages

1. Raise the temperature of the water up to 45°C and stir in the crushed malt and flakes. Stirring continuously, raise the mash temperature up to 55°C. Let it stand for half an hour and then raise the temperature again up to 66°C. Leave for 1½ hours occasionally returning the temperature back to this value.

2. Contain the mashed grain in a large grain bag to retrieve the sweet wort. Using slightly hotter water than the mash, rinse the grains to collect 4 gallons (20 litres) of extract.

3. Boil the extract with the hops for 1½ hours. Dissolve the main batch of sugar in a little hot water and add this during the boil. Also pitch in the Irish Moss as directed on the instructions.

4. Switch off the heat. Strain off the clear wort into a fermenting bin and top up to the final quantity with cold water.

5. When cool to room temperature add the yeast. Ferment in a cool place until the specific gravity falls to 1010 and rack into gallon jars or a five gallon fermenter with airlock. Apportion Gelatine finings before fitting airlocks.

6. Leave for 21 days before racking the beer from the sediment into primed beer bottles. Allow 30 days conditioning before sampling.

ELDRIDGE POPE Dorchester
THOMAS HARDY ALE

The Dorset brewers celebrated the centenary of the birth of Wessex novelist Thomas Hardy in 1969 by creating this fine brew and bottling it in old Victorian bottles. A few more batches have been produced after these treasured bottles were used.

Thomas Hardy's immortal words still apply: "It was of the most beautiful colour that the eye of an artist in beer could desire; full of body; yet brisk as a volcano; piquant, yet without a twang; luminous as an autumn sunset; free from streakiness of taste; but, finally rather heady."

Stage	2 gallons	Original gravity 1120	10 litres
1	7 lb.	Crushed pale malt	3500 gm.
1	1 lb.	Crushed lager malt	500 gm.
1	3 gallons	Water for 'barley wine' brewing	15 litres
3	1 lb.	Brewing sugar	500 gm.
3	4 oz.	Goldings hops	125 gm.
4	$\frac{1}{2}$ oz.	Wine yeast	15 gm.
6	$\frac{1}{2}$ tsp./pint	White sugar	5 ml./litre

Brewing Stages

1. Raise the temperature of the water up to 60°C and stir in the crushed malts. Stirring continuously, raise the mash temperature up to 66°C. Leave for 1$\frac{1}{2}$ hours occasionally returning the temperature back to this value.

2. Contain the mashed grain in a large grain bag to retrieve the sweet wort. Using slightly hotter water than the mash slowly and gently rinse the grains to collect 3$\frac{1}{2}$ gallons (16 litres) of extract.

3. Boil the extract with the hops and the sugar dissolved in a little water until the volume has been reduced to just over 2 gallons (10 litres). Strain off and divide equally in three gallon jars. Fit airlocks.

4. When cool add a wine yeast and ferment until the vigorous activity abates. Then siphon off into two one gallon jars, filling each to the base of the neck. Refit airlocks, and check regularly to ensure they don't dry out.

5. It will take months to complete the fermentation after which the ale should be racked again taking with it a minute quantity of the yeast sediment.

6. Store for six months before bottling in primed beer bottles and mature for 18 months before sampling.

GALES Horndean
PRIZE OLD ALE

Based on an old Yorkshire recipe, an impressively mature barley wine of the highest quality. I am yet to come across another beer that gets such careful and lavish attention by the brewery. After brewing, the naturally conditioned ale is matured in oak casks for 12 months before bottling. Even then it is recommended you keep it for another few years before sampling.

The following recipe is as near as I can get—and probably as near as I will get to this supreme ale.

Stage	2 gallons	Original gravity 1100	10 litres
1	6¼ lb.	Crushed pale malt	3250 gm.
1	1 lb.	Crushed crystal malt	500 gm.
1	1 oz.	Crushed black malt	30 gm.
1	3 gallons	Water for 'barley wine' brewing	15 litres
3	4 oz.	Molasses	125 gm.
3	3¾ oz.	Goldings hops	120 gm.
4	1 oz.	Wine yeast	30 gm.
6	½ tsp./pint	White sugar	5 ml./litre

Brewing Stages

1. Raise the temperature of the water up to 60°C and stir in the crushed malts. Stirring continuously, raise the mash temperature up to 66°C. Leave for 1½ hours occasionally returning the temperature back to this value.
2. Contain the mashed grain in a large grain bag to retrieve the sweet wort. Using slightly hotter water than the mash slowly and gently rinse the grains to collect 3½ gallons (16 litres) of extract.
3. Boil the extract with the hops and the sugar dissolved in a little water until the volume has been reduced to just over 2 gallons (10 litres). Strain off and divide equally in three gallon jars. Fit airlocks.
4. When cool add a wine yeast and ferment until the vigorous activity abates. Then siphon off into two, one gallon jars filling each to the base of the neck. Refit airlocks, and check regularly to ensure they don't dry out.
5. It will take months to complete the fermentation after which the ale should be racked again taking with it a minute quantity of the yeast sediment.
6. Store for six months before bottling in primed beer bottles and mature for 18 months before sampling.

GREENE KING Bury St. Edmunds

PALE ALE

I rate Greene King as the best brewers of bottled ales in the country sporting ten excellent, but very different and distinct ales.

The Pale Ale has a strong beautiful bouquet from the malt and hops and a luscious hoppy flavour.

Stage	5 gallons	3.4% Alcohol	25 litres
1	3 lb.	Light malt extract syrup	1500 gm.
1	12 oz.	Crushed crystal malt	400 gm.
1	1 lb.	Soft dark brown sugar	500 gm.
1	1½ oz.	Northern brewer hops	45 gm.
1	2 oz.	Goldings hops	60 gm.
1	1 tsp.	Irish moss	5 ml.
1	1 gallon	Water for 'pale ale' brewing	10 litres
2	2 oz.	Brewers yeast	60 gm.
2	½ oz.	Gelatine	15 gm.
3	½ tsp./pint	White sugar	5 ml./litre

Brewing Stages

1. Boil the malt extract, malt and hops for 45 minutes. Carefully strain off the wort from the hops and malt grains into a fermenting bin. Rinse the spent grains and hops with 2 kettlefuls of hot water. Dissolve the sugar in hot water and add this to the bin. Top up to the final quantity with cold water.

2. When cool to room temperature pitch in the yeast. Ferment 4–5 days until the activity abates. Rack off into secondary fermentation vessels and keep under airlock protection for another 7 days. Apportion gelatine finings and keep the beer under airlock protection for another 7 days.

3. Rack the beer off the sediment into primed beer bottles Allow 10 days maturation before sampling.

GREENE KING Bury St. Edmunds

STRONG PALE ALE

An impressively smooth sweetish ale that leaves no doubt about its strength!

Stage	4 gallons	Original gravity 1060	20 litres
1	7 lb.	Crushed pale malt	3500 gm.
1	8 oz.	Crushed crystal malt	250 gm.
1	2 gallons	Water for 'pale ale' brewing	10 litres
3	1 lb.	Demerara sugar	500 gm.
3	2 oz.	Molasses	60 gm.
3	3 oz.	Goldings hops	100 gm.
3	1 oz.	Northern brewer hops	30 gm.
3	1 tsp.	Irish moss	5 ml.
5	2 oz.	Brewers yeast	60 gm.
5	½ oz.	Gelatine	15 gm.
6	½ tsp./pint	White sugar	5 ml./litre

Brewing Stages

1. Raise the temperature of the water up to 60°C and stir in the crushed malts. Stirring continuously raise the mash temperature up to 66°C. Leave for 1½ hours occasionally returning the temperature back to this value.

2. Contain the mashed grain in a large grain bag to retrieve the sweet wort. Using slightly hotter water than the mash, rinse the grains to collect 4 gallons (20 litres) of extract.

3. Boil the extract with the hops for 1½ hours. Dissolve the main batch of sugar and molasses in a little hot water and add this during the boil. Also pitch in the Irish Moss as directed on the instructions.

4. Switch off the heat and strain off the clear wort into a fermenting bin and top up to the final quantity with cold water.

5. When cool to room temperature add the yeast. Ferment 4–5 days until the specific gravity falls to 1015 and rack into gallon jars or a secondary fermentation vessel, fitted with an airlock. Apportion Gelatine finings before fitting airlocks.

6. Leave for 7 days before racking the beer from the sediment into primed beer bottles. Allow 14 days conditioning before sampling.

GREENE KING Bury St. Edmunds
SUFFOLK STRONG ALE

My favourite Pale Ale of Greene King's trio. Well matured flavour and bouquet of malt. Darker in colour and less sweet than the Strong Ale version.

Stage	5 gallons	Original gravity 1060	25 litres
1	6½ lb.	Crushed pale malt	3500 gm.
1	1 lb.	Light malt extract syrup	500 gm.
1	1 oz.	Crushed black malt	30 gm.
1	3 gallons	Water for 'pale ale' brewing	15 litres
3	1 lb.	Soft dark brown sugar	500 gm.
3	2½ oz.	Goldings hops	75 gm.
3	1 oz.	Northern Brewer hops	30 gm.
3	2 oz.	Molasses	60 gm.
3	1 tsp.	Irish moss	5 ml.
4	½ oz.	Wine yeast	15 gm.
7	¼ tsp./pint	White sugar	5 ml./litre
7	3 gallons	Greene King pale ale	15 litres

Brewing Stages

1. Raise the temperature of the water up to 60°C and stir in the crushed malts. Stirring continuously, raise the mash temperature up to 66°C. Leave for 1½ hours, occasionally returning the temperature back to this value.

2. Contain the mashed grain in a large grain bag to retrieve the sweet wort. Using slightly hotter water than the mash, slowly and gently rinse the grains to collect 3 gallons (15 litres) of extract.

3. Boil the extract with the hops and the sugar dissolved in a little water until the volume has been reduced to just over 2 gallons (10 litres). Strain off and divide equally in three gallons jars. Fit airlocks.

4. When cool add a beer yeast and ferment until the vigorous activity abates. Then siphon off into two one-gallon jars, filling each to the base of the neck. Refit airlocks, and check regularly to ensure they don't dry out.

5. It will take months to complete the fermentation, after which the ale should be racked again taking with it a minute quantity of the yeast sediment.

6. Store for 18 months.

7. Rack the ale into a five gallon fermenter with airlock and add to it some freshly brewed Pale Ale (see page 54) taken after Stage 2 of that recipe. Stir thoroughly to mix the two brews and then bottle in primed beer bottles.

8. Mature for 28 days before sampling.

GREENE KING Bury St. Edmunds

HARVEST BROWN ALE

Typical Brown Ale—very dark reddy colour, medium sweetness with distinctive hops to balance the maltiness of the brew.

Stage	3 gallons	3.6% Alcohol	15 litres
1	2 lb.	D.M.S. malt extract	1000 gm.
1	2½ oz.	Crushed black malt	75 gm.
1	2 oz.	Crushed crystal malt	60 gm.
1	1 lb.	Soft dark brown sugar	500 gm.
1	1 oz.	Northern Brewer hops	30 gm.
1	1 oz.	Fuggles hops	30 gm.
1	2 gallons	Water for 'brown ale' brewing	10 litres
2	½ oz.	Home brew beer yeast	15 gm.
2	5	Saccharin tablets	5
3	½ tsp./pint	White sugar	5ml./litre

Brewing Stages

1. Boil the malt extract and hops in water for 45 minutes. Carefully strain off the wort from the hops and malt grains into a fermenting bin. Rinse the spent grains and hops with two kettlefuls of hot water. Dissolve the main batch of sugar in hot water and add this to the bin. Top up to the final quantity with cold water.

2. When cool to room temperature pitch in the yeast and saccharin tablets. Ferment 4–5 days until the activity abates. Rack off into secondary fermentation vessels and keep under airlock protection for another 7 days.

3. Rack the beer off the sediment into primed beer bottles. Allow 10 days conditioning before sampling.

HARP

HARP PILSNER

Once the best selling lager in the UK, and still the most widely distributed lager in Ireland, where sold on draught, the beer is conditioned with nitrogen to give a smooth but refreshing flavour and a nice creamy head. Canned Harp initially tastes of the can, but this off-flavour seems to dissipate quickly.

Owned by Guinness, Harp is brewed at Park Royal, as well as by several other brewers such as Morells, Greene King, Wolverhampton & Dudley, and at Dundalk and Manchester.

Stage	5 gallons	Original gravity 1034	25 litres
1	5¼ lb.	Crushed lager malt	2800 gm.
1	1 lb.	Flaked maize	500 gm.
1	3 gallons	Water for 'lager' brewing	15 litres
3	2½ oz.	Hallertau hops	75 gm.
3	1 tsp.	Irish moss	5 ml.
3	¼ tsp.	Brewers caramel	3 ml.
5	2 oz.	Lager yeast	60 gm.
5	½ oz.	Gelatine	15 gm.
6	½ tsp./pint	White sugar	5 ml./litre

Brewing Stages

1. Raise the temperature of the water up to 45°C and stir in the crushed malt and flakes. Stirring continuously, raise the mash temperature up to 55°C. Let it stand for half an hour and then raise the temperature again up to 66°C. Leave for 1½ hours occasionally returning the temperature back to this value.
2. Contain the mashed grain in a large grain bag to retrieve the sweet wort. Using slightly hotter water than the mash, rinse the grains to collect 4 gallons (20 litres) of extract.
3. Boil the extract with the hops and caramel for 1½ hours. Also pitch in the Irish Moss as directed on the instructions.
4. Switch off the heat. Strain off the clear wort into a fermenting bin and top up to the final quantity with cold water.
5. When cool to room temperature add the yeast. Ferment in a cool place until the specific gravity falls to 1010 and rack into gallon jars or a five gallon fermenter with airlock. Apportion Gelatine finings before fitting airlocks.
6. Leave for 21 days before racking the beer from the sediment into primed beer bottles. Allow 30 days conditioning before sampling. Serve chilled.

IND COOPE Burton-on-Trent

LONG LIFE

In sampling this brew I was not sure whether to classify it as a lager or a light ale. It is a very distinctive and palatable beer and that is all that really matters.

Stage	5 gallons	Original gravity 1041	25 litres
1	6 lb.	Crushed pale malt	3000 gm.
1	1½ lb.	Flaked maize	750 gm.
1	4 oz.	Wheat malt	125 gm.
1	3 gallons	Water for 'lager' brewing	15 litres
3	1 tsp.	Irish moss	5 ml.
3	1 tsp.	Brewers caramel	5 ml.
3	2 oz.	Hallertau hops	60 gm.
5	1 oz. (equiv.)	Hop extract	30 gm. (equiv.)
5	2 oz.	Lager yeast	60 gm.
5	½ oz.	Gelatine	15 gm.
6	½ tsp./pint	White sugar	5 ml./litre

Brewing Stages

1. Raise the temperature of the water up to 60°C and stir in the crushed malt and flakes. Stirring continuously, raise the mash temperature up to 66°C. Leave for 1½ hours occasionally returning the temperature back to this value.
2. Contain the mashed grain in a large grain bag to retrieve the sweet wort. Using slightly hotter water than the mash, rinse the grains to collect 4 gallons (20 litres) of extract.
3. Boil the extract with the Hallertau hops and Caramel for 1½ hours. Also pitch in the Irish Moss as directed on the instructions.
4. Switch off the heat. Strain off the clear wort into a fermenting bin and top up to the final quantity with cold water.
5. When cool to room temperature add the yeast and hop extract. Ferment in a cool place until the specific gravity falls to 1012 and rack into gallon jars or a secondary fermentation vessel, fitted with an airlock. Apportion Gelatine finings and the rest of the dry hops before fitting airlocks.
6. Leave for 14 days before racking the beer from the sediment into primed beer bottles. Allow 21 days maturation before sampling.

IND COOPE (Carlsberg–Tetley) Burton-on-Trent

LIGHT ALE

Looks more like a bitter beer and tastes are bordering on it as well.

Stage	5 gallons	3.5% Alcohol	25 litres
1	2 lb.	D.M.S. malt extract	1000 gm.
1	8 oz.	Crushed crystal malt	250 gm.
1	2 lb.	Demerara sugar	1000 gm.
1	1½ oz.	Fuggles hops	45 gm.
1	2 gallons	Water for 'light ale' brewing	10 litres
2	1 oz.	Home brew beer yeast	30 gm.
2	½ oz.	Gelatine	15 gm.
3	½ tsp./pint	White sugar	5 ml./litre

Brewing Stages

1. Boil the malt extract, crystal malt and hops in water for 45 minutes. Carefully strain off the wort from the hops and malt grains into a fermenting bin. Rinse the spent grains and hops with two kettlefuls of hot water. Dissolve the main batch of sugar in hot water and add this to the bin. Top up to the final quantity with cold water.

2. When cool to room temperature pitch in the yeast. Ferment 4–5 days until the activity abates. Rack off into secondary fermentation vessels and keep under airlock protection for another seven days. Apportion gelatine finings and keep the beer under airlock protection for another seven days.

3. Rack the beer off the sediment into primed beer bottles. Allow 10 days maturation before sampling.

McEWANS (Scottish & Newcastle)

EXPORT I.P.A.

Popular beer. Thick malty flavour kept smooth through relatively low carbonation. Nice frothy head that lasts.

Stage	5 gallons	Original gravity 1045	25 litres
1	6 lb.	Crushed pale malt	3000 gm.
1	1 lb.	Flaked barley	500 gm.
1	½ oz.	Crushed black malt	15 gm.
1	3 gallons	Water for 'pale ale' brewing	15 litres
3	1 tsp.	Irish moss	5 ml.
3	1 lb.	Soft dark brown sugar	500 gm.
3	2 oz.	Hallertau hops	60 gm.
4	1 oz. (equiv.)	Hop extract	30 gm. (equiv.)
5	2 oz.	Brewers yeast	60 gm.
5	½ oz.	Gelatine	15 gm.
6	½ tsp./pint	White sugar	5 ml./litre

Brewing Stages

1. Raise the temperature of the water up to 60°C and stir in the crushed malt and flakes. Stirring continuously, raise the mash temperature up to 66°C. Leave for 1½ hours occasionally returning the temperature back to this value.

2. Contain the mashed grain in a large grain bag to retrieve the sweet wort. Using slightly hotter water than the mash, rinse the grains to collect 4 gallons (20 litres) of extract.

3. Boil the extract with the Hallertau hops for 1½ hours. Dissolve the main batch of sugar in a little hot water and add this during the boil. Also pitch in the Irish Moss as directed on the instructions.

4. Switch off the heat and strain off the clear wort into a fermenting bin and top up to the final quantity with cold water.

5. When cool to room temperature add the yeast and hop extract. Ferment 4–5 days until the specific gravity falls to 1012 and rack into gallon jars or a five gallon fermenter with airlock. Apportion Gelatine finings before fitting airlocks.

6. Leave for 7 days before racking the beer from the sediment into primed beer bottles. Allow 10 days maturation before sampling.

SCOTTISH & NEWCASTLE

NEWCASTLE AMBER ALE

A light refreshing ale in many ways styled on the better known Brown Ale version.

Stage	5 gallons	3.2% Alcohol	25 litres
1	2½ lb.	D.M.S. malt extract	1250 gm.
1	6 oz.	Crushed crystal malt	200 gm.
1	1 lb.	Soft brown sugar	500 gm.
1	1 lb.	Amber sugar crystals	500 gm.
1	1 oz.	Fuggles hops	30 gm.
1	2 gallons	Water for 'light ale' brewing	10 litres
2	1½ oz. (equiv.)	Hop extract	45 gm. (equiv.)
2	1 oz.	Home brew beer yeast	30 gm.
2	½ oz.	Gelatine	15 gm.
3	½ tsp./pint	White sugar	5 ml./litre

Note: Amber sugar crystals are coffee sugar crystals marketed by Tate & Lyle. Other brands of coffee sugar crystals can be substituted if necessary.

Brewing Stages

1. Boil the malt extract, malt grain and hops in water for 45 minutes. Carefully strain off the wort from the hops and malt grains into a fermenting bin. Rinse the spent grains and hops with two kettlefuls of hot water. Dissolve the crystals and sugar in hot water and add this to the bin. Top up to the final quantity with cold water.

2. When cool to room temperature pitch in the yeast and hop extract. Ferment 4–5 days until the activity abates. Rack off into secondary fermentation vessels. Apportion gelatine finings and keep the beer under airlock protection for another 7 days.

3. Rack the beer off the sediment into primed beer bottles Allow 10 days maturation before sampling.

SCOTTISH & NEWCASTLE
NEWCASTLE BROWN ALE

'Geordie Champagne' as it is affectionately called, is probably the best known Northern beer. A unique brown ale, light in colour, heavy in strength and flavour and easily recognised in its clear bottles. Celebrated its 50th Jubilee in 1977.

Stage	5 gallons	Original gravity 1048	25 litres
1	7 lb.	Crushed pale malt	3500 gm.
1	8 oz.	Crushed crystal malt	250 gm.
1	3 oz.	Crushed chocolate malt	100 gm.
1	3 gallons	Water for 'strong ale' brewing	15 litres
3	1 tsp.	Irish moss	5 ml.
3	1 lb.	Soft dark brown sugar	500 gm.
3	2 oz.	Fuggles hops	60 gm.
5	5	Saccharin tablets	5
5	1½ oz. (equiv.)	Hop extract (Northern Brewer)	50 gm. (equiv.)
5	2 oz.	Brewers yeast	60 gm.
5	½ oz.	Gelatine	15 gm.
6	½ tsp./pint	White sugar	5 ml./litre

Brewing Stages

1. Raise the temperature of the water up to 60°C and stir in the crushed malts. Stirring continuously, raise the mash temperature up to 66°C. Leave for 1½ hours occasionally returning the temperature back to this value.
2. Contain the mashed grain in a large grain bag to retrieve the sweet wort. Using slightly hotter than the mash, rinse the grains to collect 4 gallons (20 litres) of extract.
3. Boil the extract with the Fuggles hops for 1½ hours. Dissolve the main batch of sugar in a little hot water and add this during the boil. Also pitch in the Irish Moss as directed on the instructions.
4. Switch off the heat and strain off the clear wort into a fermenting bin and top up to the final quantity with cold water.
5. When cool to room temperature add the yeast, hop extract and saccharin tablets. Ferment 4–5 days until the specific gravity falls to 1012 and rack into gallon jars or a five gallon fermenter with airlock. Apportion Gelatine finings before fitting airlocks.
6. Leave for 7 days before racking the beer from the sediment into primed beer bottles. Allow 14 days conditioning before sampling.

PALMERS Bridport

EXTRA STOUT

Most enjoyable stout, well balanced and tasty.

Stage	5 gallons	Original gravity 1036	25 litres
1	5 lb.	Crushed pale malt	2500 gm.
1	8 oz.	Crushed crystal malt	250 gm.
1	6 oz.	Crushed black malt	200 gm.
1	2½ gallons	Water for 'sweet stout' brewing	12 litres
3	2 oz.	Fuggles hops	60 gm.
3	1 lb.	Soft dark brown sugar	500 gm.
5	2 oz.	Brewers yeast	60 gm.
6	½ tsp./pint	White sugar	5 ml./litre

Brewing Stages

1. Raise the temperature of the water up to 60°C and stir in the crushed malts. Stirring continuously raise the mash temperature up to 66°C. Leave for 1½ hours occasionally returning the temperature back to this value.

2. Contain the mashed grain in a large grain bag to retrieve the sweet wort. Using slightly hotter water than the mash, rinse the grains to collect 4 gallons (20 litres) of extract.

3. Boil the extract with the hops for 1½ hours. Dissolve the main batch of sugar in a little hot water and add this during the boil. Also pitch in the Irish Moss as directed on the instructions.

4. Switch off the heat. Strain off the clear wort into a fermenting bin and top up to the final quantity with cold water.

5. When cool to room temperature add the yeast. Ferment 4—5 days until the specific gravity falls to 1010 and rack into gallon jars or a five gallon fermenter with airlock.

6. Leave for 7 days before racking the beer from the sediment into primed beer bottles. Allow 7 days conditioning before sampling.

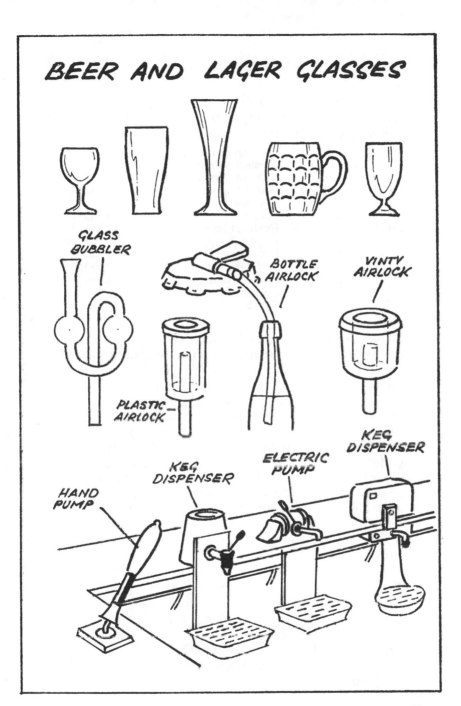

BEER AND LAGER GLASSES

GLASS
BUBBLER

PLASTIC
AIRLOCK

BOTTLE
AIRLOCK

VINTY
AIRLOCK

HAND
PUMP

KEG
DISPENSER

ELECTRIC
PUMP

KEG
DISPENSER

J. SAINSBURY PLC. (SUPERMARKET) LIGHT ALE

Excellent beery, hoppy aroma. Low carbonation level keeps the flavour smooth and plentiful without incurring too much bitterness from the generous quota of hops.

Stage	5 gallons	Original gravity 1030	25 litres
1	5 lb.	Crushed pale malt	2500 gm.
1	5 oz.	Crushed crystal malt	150 gm.
1	2½ gallons	Water for 'light ale' brewing	12 litres
3	1 oz.	Fuggles hops	30 gm.
3, 4, 5	(2 + ¼ + ¼) oz.	Goldings hops	(60 + 10 + 10) gm.
3	1 tsp.	Irish moss	5 ml.
3	6 oz.	Soft dark brown sugar	200 gm.
5	2 oz.	Brewers yeast	60 gm.
5	½ oz.	Gelatine	15 gm.
6	¼ tsp./pint	White sugar	5 ml./litre

Brewing Stages

1. Raise the temperature of the water up to 60°C and stir in the crushed malts. Stirring continuously, raise the mash temperature up to 66°C. Leave for 1½ hours occasionally returning the temperature back to this value.
2. Contain the mashed grain in a large grain bag to retrieve the sweet wort. Using slightly hotter water than the mash, rinse the grains to collect 4 gallons (20 litres) of extract.
3. Boil the extract with the Fuggles hops and the first quota of Goldings hops for 1½ hours. Dissolve the main batch of sugar in a little hot water and add this during the boil. Also pitch in the Irish Moss as directed on the instructions.
4. Switch off the heat, stir in the second batch of Goldings and allow them to soak for 15 minutes. Strain off the clear wort into a fermenting bin and top up to the final quantity with cold water.
5. When cool to room temperature add the yeast. Ferment 4—5 days until the specific gravity falls to 1010 and rack into gallon jars or a secondary fermentation vessel, fitted with an airlock. Apportion Gelatine finings and the rest of the dry hops before fitting airlocks.
6. Leave for 7 days before racking the beer from the sediment into primed beer bottles. Allow 10 days maturation before sampling.

TENNENT (BASS) Glasgow

LAGER

A good example of British lager brewing. Well hopped to give a satisfying flavour. Mind you it should be good as Tennent have been experts in Lager brewing since 1888.

Stage	5 gallons	Original gravity 1037	25 litres
1	5¼ lb.	Crushed lager malt	2700 gm.
1	8 oz.	Flaked maize	250 gm.
1	3 gallons	Water for 'lager' brewing	15 litres
3	1 tsp.	Irish moss	5 ml.
3	1 lb.	Blended honey	500 gm.
3	2 oz.	Hallertau hops	60 gm.
3	½ oz.	Goldings hops	15 gm.
5	2 oz.	Lager yeast	60 gm.
5	½ oz.	Gelatine	15 gm.
6	½ tsp./pint	White sugar	5 ml./litre

Brewing Stages

1. Raise the temperature of the water up to 45°C and stir in the crushed malt and flakes. Stirring continuously, raise the mash temperature up to 55°C. Let it stand for half an hour and then raise the temperature again up to 66°C. Leave for 1½ hours occasionally returning the temperature back to this value.

2. Contain the mashed grain in a large grain bag to retrieve the sweet wort. Using slightly hotter water than the mash, rinse the grains to collect 4 gallons (20 litres) of extract.

3. Boil the extract with the hops for 1½ hours. Dissolve the honey in a little hot water and add this during the boil. Also pitch in the Irish Moss as directed on the instructions.

4. Switch off the heat. Strain off the clear wort into a fermenting bin and top up to the final quantity with cold water.

5. When cool to room temperature add the yeast. Ferment in a cool place until the specific gravity falls to 1010 and rack into gallon jars or a five gallon fermenter with airlock. Apportion Gelatine finings before fitting airlocks.

6. Leave for 21 days before racking the beer from the sediment into primed beer bottles. Allow 30 days conditioning before sampling

TUBORG (BASS)

PILSNER LAGER

A good looking lager with a clean palate.

Stage	5 gallons	Original gravity 1031	25 litres
1	4½ lb.	Crushed lager malt	2250 gm.
1	14 oz.	Flaked maize	450 gm.
1	9 oz.	Crushed wheat malt	275 gm.
1	2½ gallons	Water for 'lager' brewing	12 litres
3	2 oz.	Hallertau hops	60 gm.
3	1 tsp.	Irish moss	5 ml.
5	2 oz.	Lager yeast	60 gm.
5	½ oz.	Gelatine	15 gm.
6	½ tsp./pint	White sugar	5 ml./lietr

Brewing Stages

1. Raise the temperature of the water up to 45°C and stir in the crushed malts and flakes. Stirring continuously, raise the mash temperature up to 55°C. Let it stand for half an hour and then raise the temperature again up to 66°C. Leave for 1 hour occasionally returning the temperature back to this value.

2. Contain the mashed grain in a large grain bag to retrieve the sweet wort. Using slightly hotter water than the mash, rinse the grains to collect 4 gallons (20 litres) of extract.

3. Boil the extract with the hops for 1½ hours. Also pitch in the Irish Moss as directed on the instructions.

4. Switch off the heat. Strain off the clear wort into a fermenting bin and top up to the final quantity with cold water.

5. When cool to room temperature add the yeast. Ferment in a cool place until the specific gravity falls to 1010 and rack into gallon jars or a secondary fermentation vessel, fitted with an airlock. Apportion Gelatine finings before fitting airlocks.

6. Leave for 21 days before racking the beer from the sediment into primed beer bottles. Allow 21 days maturation before sampling.

WATNEY MANN

WATNEYS CREAM LABEL

Rich, luscious, sweet stout.

Stage	5 gallons	3.5% Alcohol	25 litre
1	3 lb.	Malt extract syrup	1500 gm.
1	½ lb.	Crushed crystal malt	250 gm.
1	¼ lb.	Crushed black malt	250 gm.
1	1 lb.	Soft brown sugar	500 gm.
1	3 tsp.	Caramel	15 ml.
1	1½ oz.	Fuggles hops	45 gm.
1	3 gallons	Water for 'Sweet stout' brewing	15 litres
2	1 oz.	Home brew beer yeast	30 gm.
2	10	Saccharin tablets	10
3	¼ tsp./pint	White sugar	5 ml./litre

Brewing Stages

1. Boil the malt extract, grain and hops in water for 45 minutes. Carefully strain off the wort from the hops and malt grains into a fermenting bin. Rinse the spent grains and hops with two kettlefuls of hot water. Dissolve the brown sugar and caramel in hot water and add this to the bin. Top up to the final quantity with cold water.

2. When cool to room temperature pitch in the yeast and saccharin tablets. Ferment 4–5 days until the activity abates. Rack off into secondary fermentation vessels and keep under airlock protection for another 7 days.

3. Rack the beer off the sediment into primed beer bottles. Allow 7 days maturation before sampling.

WATNEY MANN

MANNS BROWN ALE

A really smooth brown ale with a delicious malt flavour.

Stage	3 gallons	3.2% Alcohol	15 litres
1	2 lb.	Malt extract syrup	1000 gm.
1	2 oz.	Crushed black malt	60 gm.
1	1 lb.	Brewing sugar	500 gm.
1	2 gallons	Water for 'brown ale' brewing	10 litres
1	2 tsp.	Caramel	10 ml.
1	½ oz.	Northern brewer hops	15 gm.
2	1 oz. (equiv.)	Hop extract	30 gm. (equiv.)
2	5	Saccharin tablets	5
3	¼ tsp./pint	White sugar	5 ml./litre

Brewing Stages

1. Boil malt extract, crushed malt and Northern Brewer hops in water for 45 minutes. Carefully strain off the wort from the hops and malt grains into a fermenting bin. Rinse the spent grains and hops with two kettlefuls of hot water. Dissolve the brewing sugar in hot water and add this to the bin. Top up to the final quantity with cold water.

2. When cool to room temperature pitch in the yeast, hop extract and saccharin tablets. Ferment 4–5 days until the activity abates. Rack off into secondary fermentation vessels and keep under airlock protection for another 7 days.

3. Rack the beer off the sediment into primed beer bottles. Allow 10 days maturation before sampling.

WHITBREAD

MACKESON

'It looks good, tastes good and by golly it does you good!'
Dark, smooth, bitter, with a tremendous amount of flavour
packed into one drink made it a firm favourite of thousands.

Stage	3 gallons	3.3% Alcohol	15 litres
1	2 lb.	Dark Malt extract	1000 gm.
1	4 oz.	Crushed chocolate malt	125 gm.
1	1 lb.	Soft dark brown sugar	500 gm.
1	4 tsp.	Brewers caramel	20 ml.
1	1 oz.	Fuggles hops	30 gm.
1	1 oz.	Northern brewer hops	30 gm.
1	2 gallons	Water for 'stout' brewing	10 litres
2	1 oz.	Home brew beer yeast	30 gm.
2	5	Saccharin tablets	5
3	$\frac{1}{2}$ tsp./pint	White sugar	5 ml./litre

Brewing Stages

1. Boil the malt extract, malt grains and hops in 2 gallons
   (10 litres) of water for 45 minutes. Carefully strain off the
   wort from the hops and malt grains into a fermenting bin.
   Rinse the spent grains and hops with two kettlefuls of hot
   water. Dissolve the caramel and sugar in hot water and add
   this to the bin. Top up to the final quantity with cold water.

2. When cool to room temperature pitch in the yeast and saccharin tablets. Ferment 4–5 days until the activity abates.
   Rack off into secondary fermentation vessels and keep
   under airlock protection for another 7 days.

3. Rack the beer off the sediment into primed beer bottles.
   Allow 10 days maturation before sampling.

WHITBREAD

HEINEKEN PILSNER LAGER

Good looking lager with a fine creamy head with a balanced hop bite.

Stage	5 gallons	Original gravity 1034	25 litres
1	5½ lb.	Crushed lager malt	2800 gm.
1	14 oz.	Flaked rice	450 gm.
1	3 oz.	Crushed crystal malt	100 gm.
1	3 gallons	Water for 'lager' brewing	15 litres
3	3 oz.	Hallertau hops	100 gm.
3	1 tsp.	Irish moss	5 ml.
5	2 oz.	Lager yeast	60 gm.
5	½ oz.	Gelatine	15 gm.
6	¼ tsp./pint	White sugar	5 ml./litre

Brewing Stages

1. Raise the temperature of the water up to 45°C and stir in the crushed malts and flakes. Stirring continuously, raise the mash temperature up to 55°C. Let it stand for half an hour and then raise the temperature again up to 66°C. Leave for 1½ hours occasionally returning the temperature back to this value.

2. Contain the mashed grain in a large grain bag to retrieve the sweet wort. Using slightly hotter water than the mash, rinse the grains to collect 4 gallons (20 litres) of extract.

3. Boil the extract with the hops for 1½ hours. Also pitch in the Irish Moss as directed on the instructions.

4. Switch off the heat. Strain off the clear wort into a fermenting bin and top up to the final quantity with cold water.

5. When cool to room temperature add the yeast. Ferment in a cool place until the specific gravity falls to 1010 and rack into gallon jars or a five-gallon fermenter with airlock. Apportion Gelatine finings before fitting airlocks.

6. Leave for 21 days before racking the beer from the sediment into primed beer bottles. Allow 30 days conditioning before sampling.

WHITBREAD

LIGHT ALE

Well balanced characteristics for a light ale. Clean, refreshing with a nice flavour from the Northern Brewer hops.

Stage	5 gallons	Original gravity 1034	25 litres
1	5 lb.	Crushed pale malt	2500 gm.
1	5 oz.	Crushed crystal malt	150 gm.
1	8 oz.	Flaked barley	250 gm.
1	2½ gallons	Water for 'light ale' brewing	12 litres
3	2 oz.	Goldings hops	60 gm.
3, 4	(¾ + ¾) oz.	Northern brewer hops	(25 + 25) gm.
3	8 oz.	Brewing sugar	250 gm.
3	1 tsp.	Irish moss	5 ml.
5	2 oz.	Brewers yeast	60 gm.
5	½ oz.	Gelatine	15 gm.
6	¼ tsp./pint	White sugar	5 ml./litre

Brewing Stages

1. Raise the temperature of the water up to 60°C and stir in the crushed malts. Stirring continuously, raise the mash temperature up to 66°C. Leave for 1½ hours occasionally returning the temperature back to this value.
2. Contain the mashed grain in a large grain bag to retrieve the sweet wort. Using slightly hotter water than the mash, rinse the grains to collect 4 gallons (20 litres) of extract.
3. Boil the extract with the Goldings hops and the first quota of Northern Brewer hops for 1½ hours. Dissolve the main batch of sugar in a little hot water and add this during the boil. Also pitch in the Irish Moss as directed on the instructions.
4. Switch off the heat, stir in the second batch of Northern Brewer hops and allow them to soak for 15 minutes. Strain off the clear wort into a fermenting bin and top up to the final quantity with cold water.
5. When cool to room temperature add the yeast. Ferment 4–5 days until the specific gravity falls to 1010 and rack into gallon jars or a five-gallon fermenter with airlock. Apportion Gelatine finings before fitting airlocks.
6. Leave for 7 days before racking the beer from the sediment into primed beer bottles. Allow 10 days maturation before sampling.

YOUNGERS Edinburgh

'WEE WILLIE' PALE ALE

Nice nutty malt flavour carefully blended with strong hops to achieve palate balance.

Stage	5 gallons	Original gravity 1036	25 litres
1	5 lb.	Crushed pale malt	2500 gm.
1	6 oz.	Flaked barley	200 gm.
1	3 gallons	Water for 'pale ale' brewing	15 litres
3	2 tsp.	Brewers caramel	10 ml.
3	2 oz.	Fuggles hops	60 gm.
3	1 oz.	Northern brewer hops	30 gm.
3	1 tsp.	Irish moss	5 ml.
3	1 lb.	Brewing sugar	500 gm.
5	2 oz.	Brewers yeast	60 gm.
5	½ oz.	Gelatine	15 gm.
6	½ tsp./pint	White sugar	5 ml./litre

Brewing Stages

1. Raise the temperature of the water up to 60°C and stir in the crushed malt and grain. Stirring continuously, raise the mash temperature up to 66°C. Leave for 1½ hours occasionally returning the temperature back to this value.
2. Contain the mashed grain in a large grain bag to retrieve the sweet wort. Using slightly hotter water than the mash, rinse the grains to collect 4 gallons (20 litres) of extract.
3. Boil the extract with the hops for 1½ hours. Dissolve the main batch of sugar and caramel in a little hot water and add this during the boil. Also pitch in the Irish Moss as directed on the instructions.
4. Switch off the heat. Strain off the clear wort into a fermenting bin and top up to the final quantity with cold water.
5. When cool to room temperature add the yeast. Ferment 4—5 days until the specific gravity falls to 1010 and rack into gallon jars or a secondary fermentation vessel, fitted with an airlock. Apportion Gelatine finings before fitting airlocks.
6. Leave for 7 days before racking the beer from the sediment into primed beer bottles. Allow 10 days maturation before sampling.

DRAUGHT BEERS REAL ALE

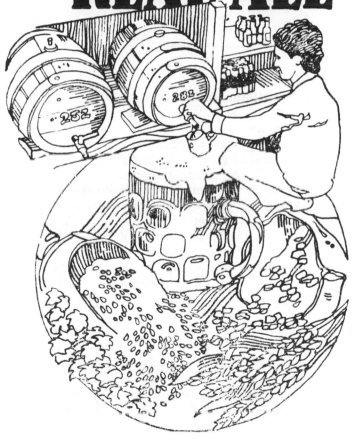

ADNAMS Southwold

SOUTHWOLD BITTER

Good malty bitter; a favourite with 'real ale' drinkers.

Stage	5 gallons	Original gravity 1037	25 litres
1	6 lb.	Crushed pale malt	3000 gm.
1	4 oz.	Crushed crystal malt	125 gm.
1	2 oz.	Crushed roast barley	60 gm.
1	3 gallons	Water for 'bitter' brewing	15 litres
3	1 tsp.	Irish moss	5 ml.
3	1 lb.	Brewing sugar	500 gm.
3	2 oz.	Fuggles hops	60 gm.
3, 4, 5	(1 + ½ + ¼) oz.	Goldings hops	(30 + 15 + 10) gm.
5	2 oz.	Brewers yeast	60 gm.
5	½ oz.	Gelatine	15 gm.
6	2 oz.	Brown sugar	60 gm.

Brewing Stages

1. Raise the temperature of the water up to 60°C and stir in the crushed malts and grain. Stirring continuously, raise the mash temperature up to 66°C. Leave for 1½ hours occasionally returning the temperature back to this value.
2. Contain the mashed grain in a large grain bag to retrieve the sweet wort. Using slightly hotter water than the mash, rinse the grains to collect 4 gallons (20 litres) of extract.
3. Boil the extract with the Fuggles hops and the first quota of Goldings hops for 1½ hours. Dissolve the main batch of sugar in a little hot water and add this during the boil. Also pitch in the Irish Moss as directed on the instructions.
4. Switch off the heat, stir in the second batch of Goldings and allow them to soak for 15 minutes. Strain off the clear wort into a fermenting bin and top up to the final quantity with cold water.
5. When cool to room temperature add the yeast. Ferment 4—5 days until the specific gravity falls to 1010 and rack into gallon jars or a five-gallon fermenter with airlock. Apportion Gelatine finings and the rest of the dry hops before fitting airlocks.
6. Leave for 7 days before racking the beer from the sediment into a primed pressure barrel. Allow 7 days conditioning before sampling.

ARKELL Swindon

B.B.B. BITTER (or 3B)

A clean, crisp, hoppy brew. After a couple of pints I acquired quite a taste for this Swindon beer. My five gallon batch went down just as well!

Stage	5 gallons	Original gravity 1039	25 litres
1	5 lb. 10 oz.	Crushed pale malt	2850 gm.
1	¾ oz.	Crushed roast barley	25 gm.
1	12 oz.	Flaked maize	400 gm.
1	3 gallons	Water for 'bitter' brewing	15 litres
3	1 tsp.	Irish moss	5 ml.
3	10 oz.	Brewing sugar	300 gm.
3	½ oz.	Bramling Cross hops	15 gm.
3	2 oz.	Fuggles hops	60 gm.
4, 5	(½ + ¼) oz.	Goldings hops	(15 + 10) gm.
5	2 oz.	Brewers yeast	60 gm.
5	½ oz.	Gelatine	15 gm.
6	2 oz.	White sugar	60 gm.

Brewing Stages

1. Raise the temperature of the water up to 60°C and stir in the crushed malt, flakes and grain. Stirring continuously, raise the mash temperature up to 66°C. Leave for 1½ hours occasionally returning the temperature back to this value.

2. Contain the mashed grain in a large grain bag to retrieve the sweet wort. Using slightly hotter water than the mash, rinse the grains to collect 4 gallons (20 litres) of extract.

3. Boil the extract with the Fuggles and Bramling Cross hops for 1½ hours. Dissolve the main batch of sugar in a little hot water and add this during the boil. Also pitch in the Irish Moss as directed on the instructions.

4. Switch off the heat, stir in the first batch of Goldings and allow them to soak for 15 minutes. Strain off the clear wort into a fermenting bin and top up to the final quantity with cold water.

5. When cool to room temperature add the yeast. Ferment 4–5 days until the specific gravity falls to 1010 and rack into gallon jars or a secondary fermentation vessel, fitted with an airlock. Apportion Gelatine finings and the rest of the dry hops

6. before fitting airlocks.
   Leave for 5 days before racking the beer from the sediment into a primed pressure barrel. Allow 5 days conditioning before sampling.

ARKELL Swindon

KINGSDOWN ALE

Bottled and draught versions are available of this light golden coloured strong ale with a warm flavour.

Stage	5 gallons	Original gravity 1060	25 litres
1	5 lb.	Crushed pale malt	2500 gm.
1	2 oz.	Crushed black malt	60 gm.
1	2½ gallons	Water for 'strong ale' brewing	12 litres
3	1 tsp.	Irish moss	5 ml.
3	4 lb.	Malt extract syrup	2000 gm.
3, 6	(14 + 2) oz.	Demerara sugar	(450 + 50) gm.
3	2 oz.	Fuggles hops	60 gm.
3	2 oz.	Goldings hops	60 gm.
5	5	Saccharin tablets	5
5	2 oz.	Brewers yeast	60 gm.
5	½ oz.	Gelatine	15 gm.

Brewing Stages

1. Raise the temperature of the water up to 60°C and stir in the crushed malts. Stirring continuously raise the mash temperature up to 66°C. Leave for 1½ hours occasionally returning the temperature back to this value.
2. Contain the mashed grain in a large grain bag to retrieve the sweet wort. Using slightly hotter water than the mash, rinse the grains to collect 4 gallons (20 litres) of extract.
3. Boil the extract with the hops for 1½ hours. Dissolve the malt extract and the main batch of sugar in a little hot water and add this during the boil. Also pitch in the Irish Moss as directed on the instructions.
4. Switch off the heat. Strain off the clear wort into a fermenting bin and top up to the final quantity with cold water.
5. When cool to room temperature add the yeast and saccharin tablets. Ferment until the specific gravity falls to 1015 and rack into gallon jars or a five gallon fermenter with an airlock. Apportion Gelatine finings before fitting airlocks.
6. Leave for 7 days before racking the beer from the sediment into a primed pressure barrel. Allow 7 days conditioning before sampling.

78

BASS WORTHINGTON Burton-on-Trent

DRAUGHT BASS

The most famous draught bitter in England, brewed at Burton-on-Trent. A really satisfying brew. Well hopped with a delicate malt flavour.

Stage	5 gallons	Original gravity 1045	25 litres
1	7 lb.	Crushed pale malt	3500 gm.
1	8 oz.	Crushed crystal malt	250 gm.
1	3 gallons	Water for 'bitter' brewing	15 litres
3	2 oz.	Fuggles hops	60 gm.
3, 4, 5	(1 + ½ + ¼) oz.	Goldings hops	(30 + 15 + 10) gm.
3	1 tsp.	Irish moss	5 ml.
3	1 lb.	Brewing sugar	500 gm.
5	2 oz.	Brewers yeast	60 gm.
5	½ oz.	Gelatine	15 gm.
6	2 oz.	Soft dark brown sugar	60 gm.

Brewing Stages

1. Raise the temperature of the water up to 60°C and stir in the crushed malts. Stirring continuously, raise the mash temperature up to 66°C. Leave for 1½ hours, occasionally returning the temperature back to this value.
2. Contain the mashed grain in a large grain bag to retrieve the sweet wort. Using slightly hotter water than the mash, rinse the grains to collect 4 gallons (20 litres) of extract.
3. Boil the extract with the Fuggles hops and the first batch of Goldings for 1½ hours. Dissolve the main batch of sugar in a little hot water and add this during the boil. Also pitch in the Irish Moss as directed on the instructions.
4. Switch off the heat, stir in the second batch of Goldings and allow them to soak for 15 minutes. Strain off the clear wort into a fermenting bin and top up to the final quantity with cold water.
5. When cool to room temperature add the yeast. Ferment 4–5 days until the specific gravity falls to 1012 and rack into gallon jars or a five-gallon fermenter with airlock. Apportion Gelatine finings and the rest of the dry hops before fitting
6. airlocks.
   Leave for 7 days before racking the beer from the sediment into a primed pressure barrel. Allow 7 days before sampling.

BRAKSPEAR Henley-on-Thames
SPECIAL BITTER
Delicious residual sweetness balances this hoppy strong brew.

Stage	5 gallons	Original gravity 1044	25 litres
1	7 lb.	Crushed pale malt	3500 gm.
1	5 oz.	Crushed crystal malt	150 gm.
1	8 oz.	Flaked maize	250 gm.
1	3 gallons	Water for 'bitter' brewing	15 litres
3	2 oz.	Molasses	60 gm.
3	1 oz.	Fuggles hops	30 gm.
3, 4, 5	(2 + ½ + ¼) oz.	Goldings hops	(60 + 15 + 10) gm.
3	8 oz.	Soft dark brown sugar	250 gm.
3	1 tsp.	Irish moss	5 ml.
5	2 oz.	Brewers yeast	60 gm.
5	½ oz.	Gelatine	15 gm.
6	2 oz.	Brown sugar	60 gm.

Brewing Stages

1. Raise the temperature of the water up to 60°C and stir in the crushed malts and flakes. Stirring continuously, raise the mash temperature up to 66°C. Leave for 1½ hour occasionally returning the temperature back to this values
2. Contain the mashed grain in a large grain bag to retrieve the sweet wort. Using slightly hotter water than the mash, rinse the grains to collect 4 gallons (20 litres) of extract.
3. Boil the extract with the Fuggles hops and the first quota of Goldings hops for 1½ hours. Dissolve the main batch of sugar and Molasses in a little hot water and add this during the boil. Also pitch in the Irish Moss as directed on the instructions.
4. Switch off the heat, stir in the second batch of Goldings and allow them to soak for 15 minutes. Strain off the clear wort into a fermenting bin and top up to the final quantity with cold water.
5. When cool to room temperature add the yeast. Ferment 4–5 days until the specific gravity falls to 1012 and rack into gallon jars or a secondary fermentation vessel, fitted with an airlock. Apportion Gelatine finings and the rest of the dry hops before fitting airlocks.
6. Leave for 7 days before racking the beer from the sediment into a primed pressure barrel. Allow 7 days conditioning before sampling.

COURAGE London

DIRECTORS BITTER

A well balanced cask conditioned brew which is rightly claimed as an old fashioned draught bitter and to be 'alive and kicking'.

Stage	5 gallons	Original gravity 1046	25 litres
1	6 lb.	Crushed pale malt	3000 gm.
1	4 oz.	Crushed crystal malt	125 gm.
1	3 gallons	Water for 'bitter' brewing	15 litres
3	1 tsp.	Irish moss	5 ml.
3	1 lb.	Barley syrup	500 gm.
3	2 oz.	Fuggles hops	60 gm.
3, 4, 5	$(1 + \frac{1}{4} + \frac{1}{4})$ oz.	Goldings hops	$(30 + 10 + 10)$ gm.
3, 6	$(14 + 2)$ oz.	Light soft brown sugar	$(450 + 50)$ gm.
5	2 oz.	Brewers yeast	60 gm.
5	$\frac{1}{2}$ oz.	Gelatine	15 gm.

Brewing Stages

1. Raise the temperature of the water up to 60°C and stir in the crushed malt and grain. Stirring continuously, raise the mash temperature up to 66°C. Leave for $1\frac{1}{2}$ hours occasionally returning the temperature back to this value.
2. Contain the mashed grain in a large grain bag to retrieve the sweet wort. Using slightly hotter water than the mash, rinse the grains to collect 4 gallons (20 litres) of extract.
3. Boil the extract with the Fuggles hops and the first quota of Goldings hops for $1\frac{1}{2}$ hours. Dissolve the main batch of sugar in a little hot water and add this during the boil. Also pitch in the Irish Moss as directed on the instructions.
4. Switch off the heat, stir in the second batch of Goldings and allow them to soak for 15 minutes. Strain off the clear Wort into a fermenting bin and top up to the final quantity with cold water.
5. When cool to room temperature add the yeast. Ferment 4–5 days until the specific gravity falls to 1012 and rack into gallon jars or a five-gallon fermenter with airlock. Apportion Gelatine finings and the rest of the dry hops before fitting airlocks.
6. Leave for 7 days before racking the beer from the sediment into a primed pressure barrel. Allow 7 days conditioning before sampling.

COURAGE Barnsley

BARNSLEY BITTER

Although no longer brewed, I thought it would be worth including a recipe for those who remember this famous beer from the Oak Well Brewery which closed in 1974.

Stage	5 gallons	Original gravity 1037	25 litres
1	5¾ lb.	Crushed pale malt	2900 gm.
1	3 oz.	Crushed crystal malt	100 gm.
1	3 oz.	Flaked maize	100 gm.
1	3 gallons	Water for 'bitter' brewing	15 litres
3	8 oz.	Brewing sugar	250 gm.
3	2 oz.	Fuggles hops	60 gm.
3, 4	(¾ + ¼) oz.	Goldings hops	(25 + 10) gm.
3	1 tsp.	Irish moss	5 ml.
3	1 tsp.	Brewers caramel	5 ml.
5	2 oz.	Brewers yeast	60 gm.
5	½ oz.	Gelatine	15 gm.
6	2 oz.	Brown sugar	60 gm.

Brewing Stages

1. Raise the temperature of the water up to 60°C and stir in the crushed malts and flakes, Stirring continuously, raise the mash temperature up to 66°C. Leave for 1½ hours occasionally returning the temperature back to this value.

2. Contain the mashed grain in a large grain bag to retrieve the sweet wort. Using slightly hotter water than the mash, rinse the grains to collect 4 gallons (20 litres) of extract.

3. Boil the extract with the Fuggles hops and the first quota of Goldings hops for 1½ hours. Dissolve the brewing sugar in a little hot water and add this during the boil. Also pitch in the Irish Moss as directed on the instructions.

4. Switch off the heat, stir in the second batch of Goldings and allow them to soak for 15 minutes. Strain off the clear wort into a fermenting bin and top up the final quantity with cold water.

5. When cool to room temperature add the yeast. Ferment 4—5 days until the specific gravity falls to 1010 and rack into gallon jars or a secondary fermentation vessel, fitted with an airlock. Apportion Gelatine finings before fitting airlocks.

6. Leave for 7 days before racking the beer from the sediment into a primed pressure barrel. Allow 7 days conditioning before sampling.

COURAGE Bristol

BEST BITTER

Hoppy, light golden amber coloured brew with a nutty malt flavour.

Stage	5 gallons	Original gravity 1040	25 litres
1	5¾ lb.	Crushed pale malt	2900 gm.
1	4 oz.	Crushed crystal malt	125 gm.
1	4 oz.	Flaked barley	125 gm.
1	3 gallons	Water for 'bitter' brewing	15 litres
3	1 tsp.	Irish moss	5 ml.
3, 6	(14 + 2) oz.	Demerara sugar	(450 + 50) gm.
3, 4	(2½ + ½) oz.	Goldings hops	(75 + 15) gm.
3	1 oz.	Northern brewer hops	30 gm.
5	2 oz.	Brewers yeast	60 gm.
5	½ oz.	Gelatine	15 gm.

Brewing Stages

1. Raise the temperature of the water up to 60°C and stir in the crushed malts and grain. Stirring continuously, raise the mash temperature up to 66°C. Leave for 1½ hours occasionally returning the temperature back to this value.
2. Contain the mashed grain in a large grain bag to retrieve the sweet wort. Using slightly hotter water than the mash, rinse the grains to collect 4 gallons (20 litres) of extract.
3. Boil the extract with the Northern Brewer hops and the first quota of Goldings hops for 1½ hours. Dissolve the main batch of sugar in a little hot water and add this during the boil. Also pitch in the Irish Moss as directed on the instructions.
4. Switch off the heat, stir in the second batch of Goldings and allow them to soak for 15 minutes. Strain off the clear wort into a fermenting bin and top up to the final quantity with cold water.
5. When cool to room temperature add the yeast. Ferment until the specific gravity falls to 1010 and rack into gallon jars or a five-gallon fermenter with airlock. Apportion Gelatine finings before fitting airlocks.
6. Leave for 7 days before racking the beer from the sediment into a primed beer pressure barrel. Allow 7 days conditioning before sampling.

DAVENPORT (Carlsberg–Tetley, Warrington)
BITTER
First class bitter. Light golden coloured brew and hoppy with a clean palate.

Stage	5 gallons	Original gravity 1039	25 litres
1	6 lb.	Crushed pale malt	3000 gm.
1	3 oz.	Crushed crystal malt	100 gm.
1	3 oz.	Crushed wheat malt	100 gm.
1	3 gallons	Water for 'bitter' brewing	15 litres
3	1 tsp.	Irish moss	5 ml.
3	2 oz.	Molasses	60 gm.
3	2½ oz.	Fuggles hops	75 gm.
3, 4, 5	(½ + ¼ + ¼) oz.	Goldings hops	(15 + 10 + 10) gm.
3, 6	(12 + 2) oz.	Light soft brown sugar	(400 + 50) gm.
5	2 oz.	Brewers yeast	60 gm.
5	¼ oz.	Gelatine	15 gm.

Brewing Stages

1. Raise the temperature of the water up to 60°C and stir in the crushed malts. Stirring continuously, raise the mash temperature up to 66°C. Leave for 1½ hours, occasionally returning the temperature back to this value.
2. Contain the mashed grain in a large grain bag to retrieve the sweet wort. Using slightly hotter water than the mash, rinse the grains to collect 4 gallons (20 litres) of extract.
3. Boil the extract with the Fuggles hops and the first quota of Goldings hops for 1½ hours. Dissolve the main batch of sugar and Molasses in a little hot water and add this during the boil. Also pitch in the Irish Moss as directed on the instructions.
4. Switch off the heat, stir in the second batch of Goldings and allow them to soak for 15 minutes. Strain off the clear wort into a fermenting bin and top up to the final quantity with cold water.
5. When cool to room temperature add the yeast. Ferment 4–5 days until the specific gravity falls to 1010 and rack into gallon jars or a secondary fermentation vessel, fitted with an airlock. Apportion Gelatine finings and the rest of the dry hops before fitting airlocks.
6. Leave for 7 days before racking the beer from the sediment into primed pressure barrel. Allow 7 days conditioning before sampling.

DONNINGTON Stow-on-the-Wold

S.B.A. BITTER

Good 'real ale' with a nice hop bite to complement the flavour of malt and roasted grain.

Stage	5 gallons	Original gravity 1040	25 litres
1	5½ lb.	Crushed pale malt	2800 gm.
1	8 oz.	Flaked barley	250 gm.
1	2 oz.	Crushed roast barley	60 gm.
1	3 gallons	Water for 'bitter' Brewing	15 litres
3	1 tsp.	Irish moss	5 ml.
3	14 oz.	Demerara sugar	450 gm.
3	2 oz.	Fuggles hops	60 gm.
3, 4, 5	(1 + ½ + ¼) oz.	Goldings hops	(30 + 15 + 10) gm.
5	2 oz.	Brewers yeast	60 gm.
5	½ oz.	Gelatine	15 gm.
6	2 oz.	Demerara sugar	60 gm.

Brewing Stages
1. Raise the temperature of the water up to 60°C and stir in the crushed malt and grain. Stirring continuously, raise the mash temperature up to 66°C. Leave for 1½ hours occasionally returning the temperature back to this value.
2. Contain the mashed grain in a large grain bag to retrieve the sweet wort. Using slightly hotter water than the mash, rinse the grains to collect 4 gallons (20 litres) of extract.
3. Boil the extract with the Fuggles hops and the first quota of Goldings hops for 1½ hours. Dissolve the main batch of sugar in a little hot water and add this during the boil. Also pitch in the Irish Moss as directed on the instructions.
4. Switch off the heat, stir in the second batch of Goldings and allow them to soak for 15 minutes. Strain off the clear wort into a fermenting bin and top up to the final quantity with cold water.
5. When cool to room temperature add the yeast. Ferment 4–5 days until the specific gravity falls to 1010 and rack into gallon jars or a five-gallon fermenter with airlock. Apportion Gelatine finings and the rest of the dry hops before fitting airlocks.
6. Leave for 7 days before racking the beer from the sediment into a primed pressure barrel. Allow 7 days conditioning before sampling.

ELDRIDGE POPE Dorchester

'ROYAL OAK'

Excellent draught Pale Ale brewed by these skilful Dorset brewers from a recipe in their brewery museum.

Stage	5 gallons	Original gravity 1048	25 litres
1	7 lb.	Crushed pale malt	3500 gm.
1	14 oz.	Flaked barley	450 gm.
1	8 oz.	Crushed crystal malt	250 gm.
1	3 gallons	Water for 'bitter' brewing	15 litres
3	1 tsp.	Irish moss	5 ml.
3	12 oz.	Soft dark brown sugar	400 gm.
3	2 oz.	Fuggles hops	60 gm.
3, 4, 5	$(1 + \frac{1}{2} + \frac{1}{4})$ oz.	Goldings hops	$(30 + 15 + 10)$ gm.
5	2 oz.	Brewers yeast	60 gm.
5	$\frac{1}{2}$ oz.	Gelatine	15 gm.

Brewing Stages

1. Raise the temperature of the water up to 60°C and stir in the crushed malt and flakes. Stirring continuously, raise the mash temperature up to 66°C. Leave for 1½ hours occasionally returning the temperature back to this value.
2. Contain the mashed grain in a large grain bag to retrieve the sweet wort. Using slightly hotter water than the mash, rinse the grains to collect 4 gallons (20 litres) of extract.
3. Boil the extract with the Fuggles hops and the first quota of Goldings hops for 1½ hours. Dissolve the main batch of sugar in a little hot water and add this during the boil. Also pitch in the Irish Moss as directed on the instructions.
4. Switch off the heat, stir in the second batch of Goldings and allow them to soak for 15 minutes. Strain off the clear wort into a fermenting bin and top up to the final quantity with cold water.
5. When cool to room temperature add the yeast. Ferment until the specific gravity falls to 1012 and rack into gallon jars or a secondary fermentation vessel, fitted with an airlock. Apportion Gelatine finings and the rest of the dry hops before fitting airlocks.
6. Leave for 7 days before racking the beer from the sediment into a primed pressure barrel. Allow 7 days conditioning before sampling.

FULLERS London

LONDON PRIDE

If I had to select just one beer to drink for the rest of my days then it would have to be 'London Pride'; a classic example of a true English Bitter Beer.

Stage	5 gallons	Original gravity 1042	25 litres
1	7 lb.	Crushed pale malt	3500 gm.
1	8 oz.	Crushed crystal malt	250 gm.
1	3 gallons	Water for 'bitter' brewing	15 litres
3	1 tsp.	Irish moss	5 ml.
3	8 oz.	Demerara sugar	250 gm.
3	1 oz.	Fuggles hops	30 gm.
3, 4, 5	$(2 + \frac{1}{2} + \frac{1}{4})$ oz.	Goldings hops	$(60 + 15 + 10)$ gm.
5	2 oz.	Brewers yeast	60 gm.
5	$\frac{1}{2}$ oz.	Gelatine	15 gm.
6	2 oz.	Demerara sugar	60 gm.

Brewing Stages

1. Raise the temperature of the water up to 60°C and stir in the crushed malts. Stirring continuously, raise the mash temperature up to 66°C. Leave for 1½ hours occasionally returning the temperature back to this value.
2. Contain the mashed grain in a large grain bag to retrieve the sweet wort. Using slightly hotter water than the mash, rinse the grains to collect 4 gallons (20 litres) of extract.
3. Boil the extract with the Fuggles hops and the first quota of Goldings hops for 1½ hours. Dissolve the main batch of sugar in a little hot water and add this during the boil. Also pitch in the Irish Moss as directed on the instructions.
4. Switch off the heat, stir in the second batch of Goldings and allow them to soak for 15 minutes. Strain off the clear wort into a fermenting bin and top up to the final quantity with cold water.
5. When cool to room temperature add the yeast. Ferment 4–5 days until the specific gravity falls to 1012 and rack into gallon jars or a five-gallon fermenter with airlock. Apportion Gelatine finings and the rest of the dry hops before fitting airlocks.
6. Leave for 7 days before racking the beer from the sediment into a primed pressure barrel. Allow 7 days conditioning before sampling.

GALES Horndean

HORNDEAN SPECIAL BITTER (H.S.B.)

A superb best bitter, well established and respected; an excellent example of true traditional brewing. It is one of the strongest bitters in the country and has a distinctive yet delicate sweetness which does not distract from the delightful hop flavour.

Stage	5 gallons	Original gravity 1051	25 litres
1	8 lb.	Crushed pale malt	4000 gm.
1	4 oz.	Crushed crystal malt	125 gm.
1	2 oz.	Crushed wheat malt	60 gm.
1	3 gallons	Water for 'bitter' brewing	15 litres
3	1 tsp.	Irish moss	5 ml.
3	3 oz.	Molasses	100 gm.
3	1 oz.	Bramling Cross hops	30 gm.
3, 4, 5	$(2 + \frac{3}{4} + \frac{1}{2})$ oz.	Goldings hops	$(60 + 25 + 15)$ gm.
3, 6	$(14 + 2)$ oz.	Soft dark brown sugar	$(450 + 50)$ gm.
5	2 oz.	Brewing yeast	60 gm.
5	$\frac{1}{2}$ oz.	Gelatine	15 gm.
5	5	Saccharin tablets	5

Brewing Stages

1. Raise the temperature of the water up to 60°C and stir in the crushed malts. Stirring continuously, raise the mash temperature up to 66°C. Leave for 1½ hours occasionally returning the temperature back to this value.

2. Contain the mashed grain in a large grain bag to retrieve the sweet wort. Using slightly hotter water than the mash, rinse the grains to collect 4 gallons (20 litres) of extract.

3. Boil the extract with the Bramling Cross hops and the first quota of Goldings hops for 1½ hours. Dissolve the main batch of sugar and molasses in a little hot water and add this during the boil. Also pitch in the Irish Moss as directed on the instructions.

4. Switch off the heat, stir in the second batch of Goldings and allow them to soak for 15 minutes. Strain off the clear wort into a fermenting bin and top up to the final quantity with cold water.

5. When cool to room temperature add the yeast and saccharin tablets. Ferment 4–5 days until the specific gravity falls to 1015 and rack into gallon jars or a secondary fermentation vessel, fitted with an airlock. Apportion Gelatine finings and the rest of the dry hops before fitting airlocks.

6. Leave for 7 days before racking the beer from the sediment into a primed pressure barrel. Allow 5 days conditioning before sampling.

Cellar Language

Stillage—Chocks and supports for beer casks.

Soft Peg—Porous peg that vents conditioning CO_2 from cask.

Ullage—space in the barrel above the beer.

Bung—Large cork fitting aperture in stave of cask.

Hard Peg—A long conical hard wood peg for insertion in vent hole of shive to exclude air.

Shive—Flat wooden plug fitting used to house pegs.

GIBB MEW Salisbury
BISHOPS TIPPLE

A dynamite brew that should be dispensed with an eye dropper to the uninitiated drinker! It is one of the strongest beers to be served on draught in Britain and is a deliciously smooth drink. Initially the extra sweetness takes some getting used to, but after a jar or so you will probably swear it to be 'fire and malt nectar' as some of my colleagues do!

Stage	4 gallons	Original gravity 1066	20 litres
1	7 lb.	Crushed pale malt	3500 gm.
1	1 lb.	Crushed crystal malt	500 gm.
1	½ oz.	Crushed black malt	15 gm.
1	3 gallons	Water for 'strong ale' brewing	15 litres
3	1 tsp.	Irish moss	5 ml.
3	1½ lb.	Golden syrup	750 gm.
3	2 oz.	Molasses	60 gm.
3	3 oz.	Goldings hops	100 gm.
5	5	Saccharin tablets	5
5	2 oz.	Brewers yeast	60 gm.
5	½ oz.	Gelatine	15 gm.
6	2 oz.	White sugar	60 gm.

Brewing Stages

1. Raise the temperature of the water up to 60°C and stir in the crushed malt. Stirring continuously, raise the mash temperature up to 66°C. Leave for 1½ hours occasionally returning the temperature back to this value.
2. Contain the mashed grain in a large grain bag to retrieve the sweet wort. Using slightly hotter water than the mash, rinse the grains to collect 4 gallons (20 litres) of extract.
3. Boil the extract with the hops for 1½ hours. Dissolve the syrup and molasses in a little hot water and add this during the boil. Also pitch in the Irish Moss as directed on the instructions.
4. Switch off the heat. Strain off the clear wort into a fermenting bin and top up to the final quantity with cold water.
5. When cool to room temperature add the yeast and saccharin tablets. Ferment until the specific gravity falls to 1020 and rack into gallon jars or a five-gallon fermenter with airlock. Apportion Gelatine finings before fitting airlocks.
6. Leave for 10 days before racking the beer from the sediment into a primed pressure barrel. Allow 10 days conditioning before sampling.

GREENE KING Bury St. Edmunds
ABBOT ALE

Full bodied, robust, well hopped ale which can be found as a draught bitter or a bottled ale. The draught version won the Champion Cup for the best draught bitter in 1968 at the International Brewers Exhibition.

Stage	5 gallons	Original gravity 1049	25 litres
1	7½ lb.	Crushed pale malt	3800 gm.
1	3 oz.	Crushed crystal malt	100 gm.
1	2 oz.	Crushed roast malt	60 gm.
1	8 oz.	Flaked maize	250 gm.
1	3 gallons	Water for 'bitter' brewing	15 litres
3	1 tsp.	Irish moss	5 ml.
3	¾ oz.	Northern brewer hops	25 gm.
3, 4, 5	(3 + ¼ + ½) oz.	Goldings hops	(100 + 15 + 10) gm
3, 6	(12 + 2) oz.	Soft dark brown sugar	(400 + 60) gm.
5	2 oz.	Brewers yeast	60 gm.
5	½ oz.	Gelatine	15 gm.

Brewing Stages

1. Raise the temperature of the water up to 60°C and stir in the crushed malts and grain. Stirring continuously raise the mash temperature up to 66°C. Leave for 1½ hours occasionally returning the temperature back to this value.
2. Contain the mashed grain in a large grain bag to retrieve the sweet wort. Using slightly hotter water than the mash, rinse the grains to collect 4 gallons (20 litres) of extract.
3. Boil the extract with the Northern Brewer hops and the first quota of Goldings hops for 1½ hours. Dissolve the main batch of sugar in a little hot water and add this during the boil. Also pitch in the Irish Moss as directed on the instructions.
4. Switch off the heat, stir in the second batch of Goldings and allow them to soak for 15 minutes. Strain off the clear wort into a fermenting bin and top up to the final quantity with cold water.
5. When cool to room temperature add the yeast. Ferment 4–5 days until the specific gravity falls to 1012 and rack into gallon jars or a secondary fermentation vessel, fitted with an airlock. Apportion Gelatine finings and the rest of the dry hops before fitting airlocks.
6. Leave for 7 days before racking the beer from the sediment into a primed pressure barrel. Allow 7 days conditioning before sampling.

HALL & WOODHOUSE Blandford Forum

BADGER BEST BITTER

A beautifully balanced beer and a good example of a best bitter.

Stage	5 gallons	Original gravity 1042	25 litres
1	5¾ lb.	Crushed pale malt	2900 gm.
1	12 oz.	Flaked maize	400 gm.
1	4 oz.	Crushed wheat malt	125 gm.
1	3 gallons	Water for 'bitter' brewing	15 litres
3	1 tsp.	Irish moss	5 ml.
3	2 oz.	Molasses	60 gm.
3	1 lb.	Brewing sugar	500 gm.
3	2 oz.	Fuggles hops	60 gm.
3, 4, 5	(1 + ¼ + ¼) oz.	Goldings hops	(30 + 10 + 10) gm.
5	½ oz.	Gelatine	15 gm.
6	2 oz.	White sugar	60 gm.

Brewing Stages

1. Raise the temperature of the water up to 60°C and stir in the crushed malts and flakes. Stirring continuously, raise the mash temperature up to 66°C. Leave for 1½ hours, occasionally returning the temperature back to this value.
2. Contain the mashed grain in a large grain bag to retrieve the sweet wort. Using slightly hotter water than the ma sh rinse the grains to collect 4 gallons (20 litres) of extract.
3. Boil the extract with the Fuggles hops and the first quota of Goldings hops for 1½ hours. Dissolve the main batch of sugar and molasses in a little hot water and add this during the boil. Also pitch in the Irish Moss as directed on the instructions.
4. Switch off the heat, stir in the second batch of Goldings and allow them to soak for 15 minutes. Strain off the clear wort into a fermenting bin and top up to the final quantity with cold water.
5. When cool to room temperature add the yeast. Ferment 4–5 days until the specific gravity falls to 1012 and rack into gallon jars or a five-gallon fermenter with airlock. Apportion Gelatine finings and the rest of the dry hops before fitting airlocks.
6. Leave for 7 days before racking the beer from the sediment into a primed pressure barrel. Allow 7 days conditioning before sampling.

HARVEY & SON LTD
SUSSEX BEST BITTER

Light golden brew with a clean palate and a predominate hop flavour.

Stage	5 gallons	Original gravity 1040	25 litres
1	6 lb.	Crushed pale malt	3000 gm.
1	8 oz.	Flaked maize	250 gm.
1	3 gallons	Water for 'bitter' brewing	15 litres
3	8 oz.	Light soft brown sugar	250 gm.
3	2 oz.	Goldings hops	60 gm.
3	1 oz.	Northern brewer hops	30 gm.
3	1 tsp.	Irish moss	5 ml.
5	2 oz.	Brewers yeast	60 gm.
5	½ oz.	Gelatine	15 gm.
6	2 oz.	Brown sugar	60 gm.

Brewing Stages

1. Raise the temperature of the water up to 60°C and stir in the crushed malt and flakes. Stirring continuously, raise the mash temperature up to 66°C. Leave for 1½ hours occasionally returning the temperature back to this value.
2. Contain the mashed grain in a large grain bag to retrieve the sweet wort. Using slightly hotter water than the mash, rinse the grains to collect 4 gallons (20 litres) of extract.
3. Boil the extract with the hops for 1½ hours. Dissolve the main batch of sugar in a little hot water and add this during the boil. Also pitch in the Irish Moss as directed on the instructions.
4. Switch off the heat, strain off the clear wort into a fermenting bin and top up to the final quantity with cold water.
5. When cool to room temperature add the yeast. Ferment 4–5 days until the specific gravity falls to 1010 and rack into gallon jars or a secondary fermentation vessel, fitted with an airlock. Apportion Gelatine finings and the rest of the dry hops before fitting airlocks.
6. Leave for 7 days before racking the beer from the sediment into a primed pressure barrel. Allow 7 days conditioning before sampling.

HOOK NORTON Banbury

'OLD HOOKY' DARK ALE

Very enjoyable well balanced brew. Like a strong mild and on a par with special bitters. I am sure there is more of a market for this style of beer.

Stage	5 gallons	Original gravity 1050	25 litres
1	7 lb.	Crushed pale malt	3500 gm.
1	3 oz.	Crushed black malt	100 gm.
1	10 oz.	Flaked barley	300 gm.
1	3 gallons	Water for 'mild ale' brewing	15 litres
3	1 tsp.	Irish moss	5 ml.
3	14 oz.	Soft dark brown sugar	450 gm.
3	2 oz.	Fuggles hops	60 gm.
3	1 oz.	Bramling Cross hops	30 gm.
5	5	Saccharin tablets	5
5	2 oz.	Brewers yeast	60 gm.
5	½ oz.	Gelatine	30 gm.
6	2 oz.	Brown sugar	60 gm.

Brewing Stages

1. Raise the temperature of the water up to 60°C and stir in the crushed malts and flakes. Stirring continuously, raise the mash temperature up to 66°C. Leave for 1½ hours, occasionally returning the temperature back to this value.
2. Contain the mashed grain in a large grain bag to retrieve the sweet wort. Using slightly hotter water than the mash, rinse the grains to collect 4 gallons (20 litres) of extract.
3. Boil the extract with the hops for 1½ hours. Dissolve the main batch of sugar in a little hot water and add this during the boil. Also pitch in the Irish Moss as directed on the instructions.
4. Switch off the heat. Strain off the clear wort into a fermenting bin and top up to the final quantity with cold water.
5. When cool to room temperature add the yeast and saccharin tablets. Ferment until the specific gravity falls to 1014 and rack into gallon jars or a five-gallon fermenter with airlock. Apportion Gelatine finings before fitting airlocks.
6. Leave for 7 days before racking the beer from the sediment into a primed pressure barrel. Allow 7 days conditioning before sampling.

IND COOPE Burton-on-Trent
BURTON ALE

Incredibly smooth ale with a nice flavour from the hops as well as bitterness. Crystal clear, with a fine creamy head, it is the best looking 'real ale' I have seen.

Stage	5 gallons	Original gravity 1048	25 litres
1	6¼ lb.	Crushed pale malt	3175 gm.
1	8 oz.	Crushed crystal malt	250 gm.
1	3 gallons	Water for 'bitter' brewing	15 litres
3	1 tsp.	Irish moss	5 ml.
3	1 lb.	Barley syrup	500 gm.
3, 6	8 + 2 oz.	Soft dark brown sugar	500 + 60 gm.
3	2 oz.	Molasses	60 gm.
3	2 oz.	Fuggles hops	60 gm.
3, 4, 5	(1½ + ¼ + ¼) oz.	Goldings hops	(45 + 10 + 10) gm.
5	2 oz.	Brewers yeast	60 gm.
5	½ oz.	Gelatine	15 gm.
5	5	Saccharin tablets	5

Brewing Stages

1. Raise the temperature of the water up to 60°C and stir in the crushed malts. Stirring continuously raise the mash temperature up to 66°C. Leave for 1½ hours occasionally returning the temperature back to this value.

2. Contain the mashed grain in a large grain bag to retrieve the sweet wort. Using slightly hotter water than the mash, rinse the grains to collect 4 gallons (20 litres) of extract.

3. Boil the extract with the Fuggles hops and the first quota of Goldings hops for 1½ hours. Dissolve the main batch of sugar, molasses and barley syrup in a little hot water and add this during the boil. Also pitch in the Irish Moss as directed on the instructions.

4. Switch off the heat, stir in the second batch of Goldings and allow them to soak for 15 minutes. Strain off the clear wort into a fermenting bin and top up to the final quantity with cold water.

5 When cool to room temperature add the yeast. Ferment until the specific gravity falls to 1012 and rack into gallon jars or a secondary fermentation vessel, fitted with an airlock. Apportion Gelatine finings and the saccharin tablets and the rest of the dry hops before fitting airlocks.

6. Leave for seven days before racking the beer from the sediment into a primed pressure barrel. Allow seven days conditioning before sampling.

KING & BARNES Horsham

SUSSEX PALE ALE

Good light bodied bitter with an excellent hop flavour. Sensible gravity for a drinking session because it is a beer you want to stay with.

Stage	5 gallons	Original gravity 1035	25 litres
1	4¾ lb.	Crushed pale malt	2400 gm.
1	1 lb.	Flaked maize	500 gm.
1	3 gallons	Water for 'bitter' brewing	15 litres
3	1 tsp.	Irish moss	5 ml.
3	6 oz.	Inverted brown sugar see page 18	200 gm.
3	2 oz.	Fuggles hops	60 gm.
3, 4, 5	(¼ + ¼ + ¼) oz.	Goldings hops	(15 + 10 + 10) gm.
5	2 oz.	Brewers yeast	60 gm.
5	½ oz.	Gelatine	15 gm.
6	2 oz.	Brown sugar	60 gm.

Brewing Stages

1. Raise the temperature of the water up to 60°C and stir in the crushed malt and flakes. Stirring continuously raise the mash temperature up to 66°C. Leave for 1½ hours occasionally returning the temperature back to this value.
2. Contain the mashed grain in a large grain bag to retrieve the sweet wort. Using slightly hotter water than the mash, rinse the grains to collect 4 gallons (20 litres) of extract.
3. Boil the extract with the Fuggles hops and the first quota of Goldings hops for 1½ hours. Dissolve the main batch of sugar in a little hot water and add this during the boil. Also pitch in the Irish Moss as directed on the instructions.
4. Switch off the heat, stir in the second batch of Goldings and allow them to soak for 15 minutes. Strain off the clear wort into a fermenting bin and top up to the final quantity with cold water.
5. When cool to room temperature add the yeast. Ferment until the specific gravity falls to 1010 and rack into gallon jars or a five-gallon fermenter with airlock. Apportion Gelatine finings and the rest of the dry hops before fitting airlocks.
6. Leave for 7 days before racking the beer from the sediment into a primed pressure barrel. Allow 5 days maturation before sampling.

KING & BARNES Horsham

MILD ALE

Enjoyable hoppy mild, a bit like a bitter beer with additional flavour from roasted malts.

Stage	5 gallons	Original gravity 1033	25 litres
1	4½ lb.	Crushed pale malt	2250 gm.
1	5 oz.	Flaked maize	150 gm.
1	3 oz.	Crushed black malt	100 gm.
1	3 gallons	Water for 'mild ale' brewing	15 litres
3	1 tsp.	Irish moss	5 ml.
3	1 lb.	Brewing sugar	500 gm.
3	1 tsp.	Brewers caramel	5 ml.
3	½ oz.	W.G.V. hops	15 gm.
3	2 oz.	Fuggles hops	60 gm.
5	2oz.	Brewers yeast	60 gm.
6	2 oz.	Brown sugar	60 gm.

Brewing Stages

1. Raise the temperature of the water up to 60°C and stir in the crushed malts and flakes. Stirring continuously, raise the mash temperature up to 66°C. Leave for 1½ hours occasionally returning the temperature back to this value.
2. Contain the mashed grain in a large grain bag to retrieve the sweet wort. Using slightly hotter water than the mash, rinse the grains to collect 4 gallons (20 litres) of extract.
3. Boil the extract with the hops for 1½ hours. Dissolve the main batch of sugar and caramel in a little hot water and add this during the boil. Also pitch in the Irish Moss as directed on the instructions.
4. Switch off the heat. Strain off the clear wort into a fermenting bin and top up to the final quantity with cold water.
5. When cool to room temperature add the yeast. Ferment 4—5 days until the specific gravity falls to 1010 and rack into gallon jars or a secondary fermentation vessel, fitted with an airlock.
6. Leave for 7 days before racking the beer from the sediment into a primed pressure barrel. Allow 7 days conditioning before sampling.

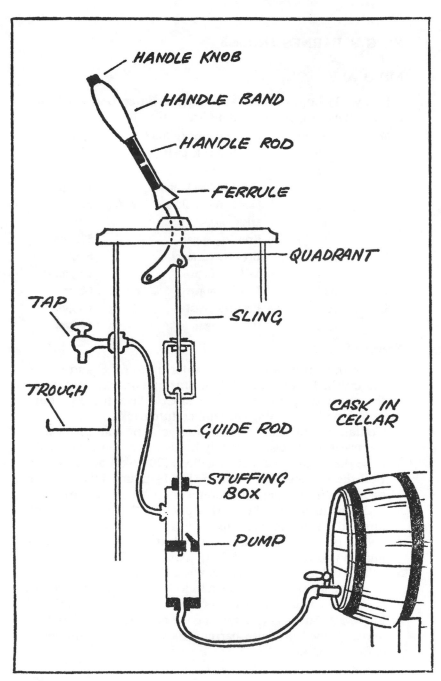

HANDLE KNOB

HANDLE BAND

HANDLE ROD

FERRULE

QUADRANT

TAP

SLING

TROUGH

GUIDE ROD

CASK IN CELLAR

STUFFING BOX

PUMP

KING & BARNES Horsham

SUSSEX OLD ALE

One of the best old ales I have tasted. Like a full bodied winey strong mild ale.

Stage	5 gallons	Original gravity 1048	25 litres
1	7¼ lb.	Crushed pale malt	3625 gm.
1	5 oz.	Crushed black malt	150 gm.
1	3 gallons	Water for 'old ale' brewing	15 litres
3	1 oz.	Molasses	30 gm.
3	3 oz.	Fuggles hops	100 gm.
3	1 oz.	W.G.V. hops	30 gm.
3, 6	(14 + 2) oz.	Soft dark brown sugar	(450 + 50) gm.
5	5	Saccharin tablets	5
5	2 oz.	Brewers yeast	60 gm.
5	¼ oz.	Gelatine	15 gm.

Brewing Stages
1. Raise the temperature of the water up to 60°C and stir in the crushed malts. Stirring continuously raise the mash temperature up to 66°C. Leave for 1½ hours occasionally returning the temperature back to this value.
2. Contain the mashed grain in a large grain bag to retrieve the sweet wort. Using slightly hotter water than the mash rinse the grains to collect 4 gallons (20 litres) of extract.
3. Boil the extract with the hops for 1½ hours. Dissolve the main batch of sugar and molasses in a little hot water and add this during the boil. Also pitch in the Irish Moss as directed on the instructions.
4. Switch off the heat, strain off the clear wort into a fermenting bin and top up to the final quantity with cold water.
5. When cool to room temperature add the yeast and saccharin tablets. Ferment until the specific gravity falls to 1012 and rack into gallon jars or a five-gallon fermenter with airlock. Apportion Gelatine finings before fitting airlocks.
6. Leave for 7 days before racking the beer from the sediment into a primed pressure barrel. Allow 7 days conditioning before sampling.

MARSTONS Burton-on-Trent

PEDIGREE BITTER

Strong, smooth thirst quenching bitter.

Stage	5 gallons	Original gravity 1044	25 litres
1	6 lb.	Crushed pale malt	3000 gm.
1	3 gallons	Water for 'bitter' brewing	15 litres
3	1 tsp.	Irish moss	5 ml.
3	1 lb.	Barley syrup	500 gm.
3	1 lb.	Brewing sugar	500 gm.
3	1 tsp.	Brewers caramel	5 ml.
3	2½ oz.	Fuggles hops	75 gm.
3	1 oz.	Goldings hops	30 gm.
5	2 oz.	Brewers yeast	60 gm.
5	½ oz.	Gelatine	15 gm.
6	2 oz.	Brown sugar	60 gm.

Brewing Stages

1. Raise the temperature of the water up to 60°C and stir in the crushed malt. Stirring continuously raise, the mash temperature up to 66°C. Leave for 1½ hours occasionally returning the temperature back to this value.
2. Contain the mashed grain in a large grain bag to retrieve the sweet wort. Using slightly hotter water than the mash, rinse the grains to collect 4 gallons (20 litres) of extract.
3. Boil the extract with the hops for 1½ hours. Dissolve the barley syrup, caramel and the main batch of sugar in a little hot water and add this during the boil. Also pitch in the Irish Moss as directed on the instructions.
4. Switch off the heat, strain off the clear wort into a fermenting bin and top up to the final quantity with cold water.
5. When cool to room temperature add the yeast. Ferment 4–5 days until the specific gravity falls to 1012 and rack into gallon jars or a secondary fermentation vessel, fitted with an airlock. Apportion Gelatine finings before fitting airlocks.
6. Leave for 7 days before racking the beer from the sediment into a primed pressure barrel. Allow 7 days conditioning before sampling.

MITCHELLS & BUTLERS (BASS)

DPA BITTER

This bitter, Dunkirk Pale Ale, is often served as a light mild ale and called Derby Pale Ale!

Stage	5 gallons	Original gravity 1033	25 litres
1	4¼ lb.	Crushed pale malt	2200 gm.
1	10 oz.	Flaked maize	300 gm.
1	2½ gallons	Water for 'light ale' brewing	12 litres
3	1 tsp.	Irish moss	5 ml.
3	14 oz.	Demerara sugar	450 gm.
3	2 oz.	Fuggles hops	60 gm.
5	2 oz.	Brewers yeast	60 gm.
5	½ oz.	Gelatine	15 gm.
6	2 oz.	Demerara sugar	60 gm.

Brewing Stages

1. Raise the temperature of the water up to 60°C and stir in the crushed malt and flakes. Stirring continuously, raise the mash temperature up to 66°C. Leave for 1½ hours occasionally returning the temperature back to this value.
2. Contain the mashed grain in a large grain bag to retrieve the sweet wort. Using slightly hotter water than the mash, rinse the grains to collect 4 gallons (20 litres) of extract.
3. Boil the extract with the hops for 1½ hours. Dissolve the main batch of sugar in a little hot water and add this during the boil. Also pitch in the Irish Moss as directed on the instructions.
4. Switch off the heat, strain off the clear wort into a fermenting bin and top up to the final quantity with cold water.
5. When cool to room temperature add the yeast. Ferment 4–5 days until the specific gravity falls to 1010 and rack into gallon jars or a five-gallon fermenter with airlock. Apportion Gelatine finings before fitting airlocks.
6. Leave for 7 days before racking the beer from the sediment into a primed pressure barrel. Allow 7 days conditioning before sampling.

MORLAND Abingdon
BEST BITTER

Lovely hop flavour blended with real expertise in this full malty brew. Now replaced by an improved beer, 'Old Masters'.

Stage	5 gallons	Original gravity 1043	25 litres
1	7 lb.	Crushed pale malt	3500 gm.
1	4 oz.	Crushed crystal malt	125 gm.
1	3 gallons	Water for 'bitter' brewing	15 litres
3	1 tsp.	Irish moss	5 ml.
3	½ oz.	Fuggles hops	15 gm.
3	½ oz.	Bramling Cross hops	15 gm.
3, 4, 5	(2 + ½ + ¼) oz.	East Kent Goldings hops	(60 + 15 + 10) gm.
3, 6	(12 + 2) oz.	Soft dark brown sugar	(400 + 50) gm.
5	2 oz.	Brewers yeast	60 gm.
5	½ oz.	Gelatine	15 gm.

Brewing Stages

1. Raise the temperature of the water up to 60°C and stir in the crushed malt and grain. Stirring continuously, raise the mash temperature up to 66°C. Leave for 1½ hours, occasionally returning the temperature back to this value.
2. Contain the mashed grain in a large grain bag to retrieve the sweet wort. Using slightly hotter water than the mash, rinse the grains to collect 4 gallons (20 litres) of extract.
3. Boil the extract with the Fuggles and Bramling Cross hops and the first quota of Goldings hops for 1½ hours. Dissolve the main batch of sugar in a little hot water and add this during the boil. Also pitch in the Irish Moss as directed on the instructions.
4. Switch off the heat, stir in the second batch of Goldings and allow them to soak for 15 minutes. Strain off the clear wort into a fermenting bin and top up to the final quantity with cold water.
5. When cool to room temperature add the yeast. Ferment 4–5 days until the specific gravity falls to 1012 and rack into gallon jars or a secondary fermentation vessel, fitted with an airlock. Apportion Gelatine finings and the rest of the dry hops before fitting airlocks.
6. Leave for 7 days before racking the beer from the sediment into a primed pressure barrel. Allow 7 days conditioning before sampling.

102

MORLAND Abingdon
MILD ALE

I was very impressed with this brew. A particularly good example of mild ale. Called 'Ale' locally. Production stopped some time ago, and it has recently been replaced by a new mild beer, 'Revival Mild', which is selling well.

Stage	5 gallons	Original gravity 1033	25 litres
1	5 lb.	Crushed pale malt	2500 gm.
1	4 oz.	Crushed roast barley	125 gm.
1	2½ gallons	Water for 'mild ale' brewing	12 litres
3	1 tsp.	Irish moss	5 ml.
3	2 oz.	Fuggles hops	60 gm.
3, 6	(12 + 2) oz.	Soft dark brown sugar	(400 + 50) gm.
5	2 oz.	Brewers yeast	60 gm.

Brewing Stages

1. Raise the temperature of the water up to 60°C and stir in the crushed malt and grain. Stirring continuously, raise the mash temperature up to 66°C. Leave for 1½ hours, occasionally returning the temperature back to this value.

2. Contain the mashed grain in a large grain bag to retrieve the sweet wort. Using slightly hotter water than the mash, rinse the grains to collect 4 gallons (20 litres) of extract.

3. Boil the extract with the hops for 1½ hours. Dissolve the main batch of sugar in a little hot water and add this during the boil. Also pitch in the Irish Moss as directed on the instructions.
   Switch off the heat, strain off the clear wort into a fermenting bin and top up to the final quantity with cold water.

5. When cool to room temperature add the yeast. Ferment 4–5 days until the specific gravity falls to 1010 and rack into gallon jars or a five-gallon fermenter with airlock.

6. Leave for 7 days before racking the beer from the sediment into a primed pressure barrel. Allow 7 days conditioning before sampling.

103

MORRELL Oxford

VARSITY BITTER

Good best bitter; well balanced and malty.

Stage	5 gallons	Original gravity 1041	25 litres
1	5¾ lb.	Crushed pale malt	2900 gm.
1	8 oz.	Crushed crystal malt	250 gm.
1	1 oz.	Crushed roast barley	30 gm.
1	3 gallons	Water for 'bitter' brewing	15 litres
3	1 tsp.	Irish moss	5 ml.
3	14 oz.	Demerara sugar	450 gm.
3	3 oz.	Fuggles hops	100 gm.
5	2 oz.	Brewers yeast	60 gm.
5	½ oz.	Gelatine	15 gm.
6	2 oz.	Demerara sugar	60 gm.

Brewing Stages

1. Raise the temperature of the water up to 60°C and stir in the crushed malts and grain. Stirring continuously, raise the mash temperature up to 66°C. Leave for 1½ hours, occasionally returning the temperature back to this value.

2. Contain the mashed grain in a large grain bag to retrieve the sweet wort. Using slightly hotter water than the mash, rinse the grains to collect 4 gallons (20 litres) of extract.

3. Boil the extract with the hops for 1½ hours. Dissolve the main batch of sugar in a little hot water and add this during the boil. Also pitch in the Irish Moss as directed on the instructions.

4. Switch off the heat, strain off the clear wort into a fermenting bin and top up to the final quantity with cold water.

5. When cool to room temperature add the yeast. Ferment 4–5 days until the specific gravity falls to 1010 and rack into gallon jars or a five-gallon fermenter with airlock. Apportion gelatine finings before fitting airlocks.

6. Leave for 7 days before racking the beer from the sediment into a primed pressure barrel. Allow 7 days conditioning before sampling.

PAINE St. Neots
E.G. BITTER

This brewery has been closed for several years, but is survived by Paines Malt Ltd, makers of the famous 'John Bull' beer kits. Eynesbury Giant or Extra Gravity was a full bodied sweetish malty brew with a beautiful 'sugary' bouquet.

Stage	5 gallons	Original gravity 1049	25 litres
1	7¼ lb.	Crushed pale malt	3625 gm.
1	1 lb.	Light soft brown sugar	500 gm.
1	3 gallons	Water for 'bitter' brewing	15 litres
3	1 tsp.	Irish moss	5 ml.
3	2 oz.	Fuggles hops	60 gm.
3	1½ oz.	Goldings hops	45 gm.
3, 6	(2 + 1) oz.	Black treacle	(60 + 30) gm.
5	5	Saccharin tablets	5
5	2 oz.	Brewers yeast	60 gm.
5	¼ oz.	Gelatine	15 gm.
6	1 oz.	Brown sugar	30 gm.

Brewing Stages

1. Raise the temperature of the water up to 60°C and stir in the crushed malt. Stirring continuously, raise the mash temperature up to 66°C. Leave for 1½ hours, occasionally returning the temperature back to this value.

2. Contain the mashed grain in a large grain bag to retrieve the sweet wort. Using slightly hotter water than the mash, rinse the grains to collect 4 gallons (20 litres) of extract.

3. Boil the extract with the hops for 1½ hours. Dissolve the main batch of sugar and treacle in a little hot water and add this during the boil. Also pitch in the Irish Moss as directed on the instructions.

4. Switch off the heat, strain off the clear wort into a fermenting bin and top up to the final quantity with cold water.

5. When cool to room temperature add the yeast and saccharin tablets. Ferment 4—5 days until the specific gravity falls to 1012 and rack into gallon jars or a secondary fermentation vessel, fitted with an airlock. Apportion Gelatine finings before fitting airlocks.

6. Leave for 7 days before racking the beer from the sediment into a primed pressure barrel. Allow 7 days conditioning before sampling.

PALMERS Bridport

DRAUGHT I.P.A.

A most impressive pale ale with a first class hop flavour. Deserves far more recognition.

Stage	5 gallons	Original gravity 1040	25 litres
1	6 lb.	Crushed pale malt	3000 gm.
1	2 oz.	Crushed roast barley	60 gm.
1	3 gallons	Water for 'bitter' brewing	15 litres
3	1 tsp.	Irish moss	5 ml.
3	1 lb.	Brewing sugar	500 gm.
3	1 oz.	Molasses	30 gm.
3	1¼ oz.	Fuggles hops	40 gm.
3, 4, 5	(2 + ¼ + ¼) oz.	Goldings hops	(60 + 10 + 10) gm.
5	2 oz.	Brewers yeast	60 gm.
5	½ oz.	Gelatine	15 gm.
6	2 oz.	Brown sugar	60 gm.

Brewing Stages

1. Raise the temperature of the water up to 60°C and stir in the crushed malt and grain. Stirring continuously, raise the mash temperature up to 66°C. Leave for 1½ hours, occasionally returning the temperature back to this value.
2. Contain the mashed grain in a large grain bag to retrieve the sweet wort. Using slightly hotter water than the mash, rinse the grains to collect 4 gallons (20 litres) of extract.
3. Boil the extract with the Fuggles hops and the first quota of Goldings hops for 1½ hours. Dissolve the main batch of sugar and molasses in a little hot water and add this during the boil. Also pitch in the Irish Moss as directed on the instructions.
4. Switch off the heat, stir in the second batch of Goldings and allow them to soak for 15 minutes. Strain off the clear wort into a fermenting bin and top up to the final quantity with cold water.
5. When cool to room temperature add the yeast. Ferment 4–5 days until the specific gravity falls to 1010 and rack into gallon jars or a five-gallon fermenter with airlock. Apportion Gelatine finings and the rest of the dry hops before fitting airlocks.
6. Leave for 7 days before racking the beer from the sediment into a primed pressure barrel. Allow 7 days conditioning before sampling.

RUDDLES Oakham

COUNTY BITTER

A robust bitter packed with the flavour of malt and hops.

Stage	5 gallons	Original gravity 1050	25 litres
1	7¾ lb.	Crushed pale malt	3875 gm.
1	8 oz.	Crushed crystal malt	250 gm.
1	3 gallons	Water for 'bitter' brewing	15 litres
3	1 tsp.	Irish moss	5 ml.
3	1 lb.	Brewing sugar	500 gm.
3	1 oz.	Molasses	30 gm.
3	2 tsp.	Brewers caramel	10 ml.
3	2 oz.	Fuggles hops	60 gm.
3, 4	(1½ + ½) oz.	W.G.V. hops	(45 + 15) gm.
5	2 oz.	Brewers yeast	60 gm.
5	½ oz.	Gelatine	15 gm.
6	2 oz.	Brown sugar	60 gm.

Brewing Stages

1. Raise the temperature of the water up to 60°C and stir in the crushed malts. Stirring continuously raise, the mash temperature up to 66°C. Leave for 1½ hours, occasionally returning the temperature back to this value.
2. Contain the mashed grain in a large grain bag to retrieve the sweet wort. Using slightly hotter water than the mash, rinse the grains to collect 4 gallons (20 litres) of extract.
3. Boil the extract with the Fuggles hops and the first quota of W.G.V. hops for 1½ hours. Dissolve the main batch of sugar, molasses and caramel in a little hot water and add this during the boil. Also pitch in the Irish Moss as directed on the instructions.
4. Switch off the heat, stir in the second batch of W.G.V. hops and allow them to soak for 15 minutes. Strain off the clear wort into a fermenting bin and top up to the final quantity with cold water.
5. When cool to room temperature add the yeast. Ferment 4–5 days until the specific gravity falls to 1015 and rack into gallon jars or a secondary fermentation vessel, fitted with an airlock. Apportion Gelatine finings before fitting airlocks.
6. Leave for 7 days before racking the beer from the sediment into a primed pressure barrel. Allow 7 days conditioning before sampling.

SAMUEL SMITH Tadcaster

OLD BREWERY BITTER

Strong bitter with a light golden colour and unusual but very pleasant cask malt flavour.

Stage	5 gallons	Original gravity 1040	25 litres
1	6 lb.	Crushed pale malt	3000 gm.
1	8 oz.	Torrefied barley	250 gm.
1	6 oz.	Crushed crystal malt	200 gm.
1	3 gallons	Water for 'bitter' brewing	15 litres
3	1 tsp.	Irish moss	5 ml.
3	8 oz.	Brewing sugar	250 gm.
3	2 oz.	Molasses	60 gm.
3	2½ oz.	Fuggles hops	75 gm.
3	½ oz.	Goldings hops	15 gm.
5	2 oz.	Brewers yeast	60 gm.
5	½ oz.	Gelatine	15 gm.
6	2 oz.	Brown sugar	60 gm.

Brewing Stages

1. Raise the temperature of the water up to 60°C and stir in the crushed malts and grain. Stirring continuously, raise the mash temperature up to 66°C. Leave for 1½ hours, occasionally returning the temperature back to this value.

2. Contain mashed grain in a large grain bag to retrieve the sweet wort. Using slightly hotter water than the mash, rinse the grains to collect 4 gallons (20 litres) of extract.

3. Boil the extract with the hops for 1½ hours. Dissolve the main batch of sugar and Molasses in a little hot water and add this during the boil. Also pitch in the Irish Moss as directed on the instructions.

4. Switch off the heat, strain off the clear wort into a fermenting bin and top up to the final quantity with cold water.

5. When cool to room temperature add the yeast. Ferment 4—5 days until the specific gravity falls to 1010 and rack into gallon jars or a five-gallon fermenter with airlock. Apportion Gelatine finings before fitting airlocks.

6. Leave for 7 days before racking the beer from the sediment into a primed pressure barrel. Allow 7 days conditioning before sampling.

SHEPHERD NEAME Faversham
BEST BITTER

Smoky malt flavour makes it the most easily recognised bitter in the country as well as being one of the best.

Stage	5 gallons	Original gravity 1040	25 litres
1	6 lb.	Crushed pale malt	3000 gm.
1	6 oz.	Flaked maize	200 gm.
1	6 oz.	Crushed amber malt	200 gm.
1	3 gallons	Water for 'bitter' brewing	15 litres
3	1 tsp.	Irish moss	5 ml.
3	8 oz.	Soft dark brown sugar	250 gm.
3	1 oz.	W.G.V. hops	30 gm.
3, 4, 5	$(1 + \frac{1}{4} + \frac{1}{4})$ oz.	Goldings hops	$(60 + 10 + 10)$ gm.
5	2 oz.	Brewers yeast	60 gm.
5	$\frac{1}{2}$ oz.	Gelatine	15 gm.
6	2 oz.	Brown sugar	60 gm.

Brewing Stages

1. Raise the temperature of the water up to 60°C and stir in the crushed malts and flakes. Stirring continuously, raise the mash temperature up to 66°C. Leave for 1½ hours, occasionally returning the temperature back to this value.
2. Contain the mashed grain in a large grain bag to retrieve the sweet wort. Using slightly hotter water than the mash, rinse the grains to collect 4 gallons (20 litres) of extract.
3. Boil the extract with the W.G.V. hops and the first quota of Goldings hops for 1½ hours. Dissolve the main batch of sugar in a little hot water and add this during the boil. Also pitch in the Irish Moss as directed on the instructions.
4. Switch off the heat, stir in the second batch of Goldings and allow them to soak for 15 minutes. Strain off the clear wort into a fermenting bin and top up to the final quantity with cold water.
5. When cool to room temperature add the yeast. Ferment 4–5 days until the specific gravity falls to 1010 and rack into gallon jars or a secondary fermentation vessel, fitted with an airlock. Apportion Gelatine finings and the rest of the dry hops before fitting airlocks.
6. Leave for 7 days before racking the beer from the sediment into a primed pressure barrel. Allow 7 days conditioning before sampling.

TETLEY Leeds

BITTER

A creamy smooth well balanced bitter that deserves its loyal following of the Tetley Bittermen. As a southerner, used to flat beer, my remark to the locals that their treasured brew had more froth than a lemon meringue pie was greeted with as much enthusiasm as the call for time! After a few pints I too found this typical northern styled beer very palatable indeed.

Stage	5 gallons	Original gravity 1036	25 litres
1	4¾ lb.	Crushed pale malt	2400 gm.
1	6 oz.	Crushed crystal malt	200 gm.
1	6 oz.	Crushed wheat malt	200 gm.
1	3 gallons	Water for 'bitter' brewing	15 litres
3	1 tsp.	Irish moss	5 ml.
3	1 lb.	Light soft brown sugar	500 gm.
3	2½ oz.	Fuggles hops	75 gm.
3	½ oz.	Bramling Cross hops	15 gm.
5	2 oz.	Brewers yeast	60 gm.
5	½ oz.	Gelatine	15 gm.
6	1 oz.	Brown sugar	30 gm.

Brewing Stages

1. Raise the temperature of the water up to 60°C and stir in the crushed malts. Stirring continuously, raise the mash temperature up to 66°C. Leave for 1½ hours, occasionally returning the temperature back to this value.
2. Contain the mashed grain in a large grain bag to retrieve the sweet wort. Using slightly hotter water than the mash, rinse the grains to collect 4 gallons (20 litres) of extract.
3. Boil the extract with the hops for 1½ hours. Dissolve the main batch of sugar in a little hot water and add this during the boil. Also pitch in the Irish Moss as directed on the instructions.
4. Switch off the heat, strain off the clear wort into a fermenting bin and top up to the final quantity with cold water.
5. When cool to room temperature add the yeast. Ferment 4–5 days until the specific gravity falls to 1010 and rack into gallon jars or a five-gallon fermenter with airlock. Apportion gelatine finings before fitting airlocks.
6. Leave for 7 days before racking the beer from the sediment into a primed pressure barrel. Allow 7 days conditioning before sampling.

THEAKSTONS Masham and Newcastle

'OLD PECULIER'

Aptly named, this brew is unusual, very distinct, but pleasantly peculiar. The dark brew owes much of its charm to the bouquet, flavour and after taste of the priming sugars. My notes record it as one of the best dark draught beers I have tasted and a good example of an old fashioned ale.

Stage	5 gallons	6% Alcohol	25 litres
1	3 gallons	Water for 'brown ale' brewing	15 litres
1	4 lb.	Dark malt extract	2000 gm.
1	8 oz.	Crushed roast barley	250 gm.
1	8 oz.	Crushed crystal malt	250 gm.
1	2 lb.	Soft dark brown sugar	1000 gm.
1	2 oz.	Fuggles hops	60 gm.
2	5	Saccharin tablets	5
2	2 oz.	Brewers yeast	60 gm.
3	3 oz.	Black treacle	100 gm.

Brewing Stages

1. Boil the malt extract, malt grains and hops in water for 45 minutes. Carefully strain off the wort from the hops and malt grains into a fermenting bin. Rinse the spent grains and hops with two kettlefuls of hot water. Dissolve the main quota of sugar in hot water and add this to the bin. Top up to the final quantity with cold water.

2. When cool to room temperature pitch in the yeast and saccharin tablets. Ferment until the activity abates. Rack off into secondary fermentation vessels and keep under airlock protection for another 7 days.

3. Rack the beer from the sediment into a barrel primed with treacle. Allow 7 days conditioning before sampling.

THEAKSTONS Masham and Newcastle

BEST BITTER

A good 'real ale'. Very light coloured but with ample malt body to balance the hops. If you can get some of the brewery yeast so much the better, as this ale benefits from the slight yeast flavour.

Stage	5 gallons	Original gravity 1038	25 litres
1	5½ lb.	Crushed pale malt	2800 gm.
1	12 oz.	Flaked maize	400 gm.
1	3 gallons	Water for 'bitter' brewing	15 litres
3	1 tsp.	Irish moss	5 ml.
3	6 oz.	Demerara sugar	200 gm.
3	2 oz.	Fuggles hops	60 gm.
3, 4, 5	(1 + ½ + ¼) oz.	Goldings hops	(30 + 15 + 10) gm.
5	2 oz.	Brewing yeast	60 gm.
5	½ oz.	Gelatine	15 gm.
6	2 oz.	Soft dark brown sugar	60 gm.

Brewing Stages

1. Raise the temperature of the water up to 60°C and stir in the crushed malt. Stirring continuously, raise the mash temperature up to 66°C. Leave for 1½ hours, occasionally returning the temperature back to this value.
2. Contain the mashed grain in a large grain bag to retrieve the sweet wort. Using slightly hotter water than the mash, rinse the grains to collect 4 gallons (20 litres) of extract.
3. Boil the extract with the Fuggles hops and the first quota of Goldings hops for 1½ hours. Dissolve the main batch of sugar in a little hot water and add this during the boil. Also pitch in the Irish Moss as directed on the instructions.
4. Switch off the heat, stir in the second batch of Goldings and allow them to soak for 15 minutes. Strain off the clear wort into a fermenting bin and top up to the final quantity with cold water.
5. When cool to room temperature add the yeast. Ferment 4–5 days until the specific gravity falls to 1010 and rack into gallon jars or a five gallon fermenter with an airlock. Apportion Gelatine finings and the rest of the dry hops before fitting airlocks.
6. Leave for 7 days before racking the beer from the sediment into a primed pressure barrel. Allow 7 days conditioning before sampling.

TOLLY COBBOLD Ipswich

BITTER

Full flavoured bitter for its gravity, smooth and very tasty.

Stage	5 gallons	Original gravity 1035	25 litres
1	2½ gallons	Water for 'bitter' brewing	12 litres
1	1 lb.	Wheat flour	500 gm.
2	4¾ lb.	Crushed pale malt	2400 gm.
2	4 oz.	Crushed crystal malt	125 gm.
4	1 tsp.	Irish moss	5 ml.
4	2 oz.	Fuggles hops	60 gm.
4, 5	(¾ + ¼) oz.	Goldings hops	(25 + 10) gm.
4, 7	(8 + 2) oz.	Soft dark brown sugar	(250 + 50) gm.
6	2 oz.	Brewers yeast	60 gm.
6	¼ oz.	Gelatine	15 gm.

Brewing Stages

1. Mix the wheat flour as a paste before thoroughly dissolving it in the cold water for mashing.
2. Raise the temperature of the water up to 60°C and stir in the crushed malt and grain. Stirring continuously, raise the mash temperature up to 66°C. Leave for 1½ hours occasionally returning the temperature back to this value.
3. Contain the mashed grain in a large grain bag to retrieve the sweet wort. Using slightly hotter water than the mash, rinse the grains to collect 4 gallons (20 litres) of extract.
4. Boil the extract with the Fuggles hops and the first quota of Goldings hops for 1½ hours. Dissolve the main batch of sugar in a little hot water and add this during the boil. Also pitch in the Irish Moss as directed on the instructions.
5. Switch off the heat, stir in the second batch of Goldings and allow them to soak for 15 minutes. Strain off the clear wort into a fermenting bin and top up to the final quantity with cold water.
6. When cool to room temperature add the yeast. Ferment 4–5 days until the specific gravity falls to 1010 and rack into gallon jars or a secondary fermentation vessel, fitted with an airlock. Apportion Gelatine finings before fitting airlocks.
7. Leave for 7 days before racking the beer from the sediment into a primed pressure barrel. Allow 7 days conditioning before sampling.

USHER Trowbridge

USHERS 'P.A.'

A light refreshing bitter.

Stage	5 gallons	Original gravity 1032	25 litres
1	4 lb. 8 oz.	Crushed pale malt	2250 gm.
1	14 oz.	Flaked maize	450 gm.
1	2½ gallons	Water for 'bitter' brewing	12 litres
3	1 tsp.	Irish moss	5 ml.
3	12 oz.	Brewing sugar	400 gm.
3	3 oz.	Fuggles hops	100 gm.
5	2 oz.	Brewers yeast	60 gm.
5	½ oz.	Gelatine	15 gm.
6	2 oz.	Brown sugar	60 gm.

Brewing Stages

1. Raise the temperature of the water up to 60°C and stir in the crushed malt and flakes. Stirring continuously, raise the mash temperature up to 66°C. Leave for 1½ hours, occasionally returning the temperature back to this value.

2. Contain the mashed grain in a large grain bag to retrieve the sweet wort. Using slightly hotter water than the mash, rinse the grains to collect 4 gallons (20 litres) of extract.

3. Boil the extract with the hops for 1½ hours. Dissolve the main batch of sugar in a little hot water and add this during the boil. Also pitch in the Irish Moss as directed on the instructions.

4. Switch off the heat, strain off the clear wort into a fermenting bin and top up to the final quantity with cold water.

5. When cool to room temperature add the yeast. Ferment 4–5 days until the specific gravity falls to 1010 and rack into gallon jars or a five gallon fermenter with an airlock. Apportion Gelatine finings before fitting airlocks.

6. Leave for 7 days before racking the beer from the sediment into a primed pressure barrel. Allow 7 days conditioning before sampling.

WADWORTH Devizes

6X BITTER

A nice light coloured hoppy brew.

Stage	5 gallons	Original gravity 1040	25 litres
1	5¼ lb.	Crushed pale malt	2700 gm.
1	12 oz.	Flaked maize	400 gm.
1	8 oz.	Crushed crystal malt	250 gm.
1	3 gallons	Water for 'bitter' brewing	15 litres
3	1 tsp.	Irish moss	5 ml.
3	10 oz.	Brewing sugar	300 gm.
3	2 oz.	Goldings hops	60 gm.
3	1 oz.	Bramling Cross hops	30 gm.
5	2 oz.	Brewers yeast	60 gm.
5	½ oz.	Gelatine	15 gm.
6	2 oz.	Brown sugar	60 gm.

Brewing Stages

1. Raise the temperature of the water up to 60°C and stir in the crushed malts and flakes. Stirring continuously, raise the mash temperature up to 66°C. Leave for 1½ hours, occasionally returning the temperature back to this value.
2. Contain the mashed grain in a large grain bag to retrieve the sweet wort. Using slightly hotter water than the mash, rinse the grains to collect 4 gallons (20 litres) of extract.
3. Boil the extract with the hops for 1½ hours. Dissolve the main batch of sugar in a little hot water and add this during the boil. Also pitch in the Irish Moss as directed on the instructions.
4. Switch off the heat, strain off the clear wort into a fermenting bin and top up to the final quantity with cold water.
5. When cool to room temperature add the yeast. Ferment 4–5 days until the specific gravity falls to 1010 and rack into gallon jars or a secondary fermentation vessel, fitted with an airlock. Apportion Gelatine finings before fitting airlocks.
6. Leave for 7 days before racking the beer from the sediment into a primed pressure barrel. Allow 7 days conditioning before sampling.

WADWORTHS Devizes

OLD TIMER

Generous malty brew that is deceptively strong—as I found to my pleasure!

Stage	5 gallons	Original gravity 1054	25 litres
1	7½ lb.	Crushed pale malt	3750 gm.
1	4 oz.	Crushed crystal malt	125 gm.
1	12 oz.	Flaked barley	400 gm.
1	3 gallons	Water for 'bitter' brewing	15 litres
3	1 tsp.	Irish moss	5 ml.
3	1 lb.	Brewing sugar	500 gm.
3	2 oz.	Fuggles hops	60 gm.
3, 4, 5	(1 + ½ + ¼) oz.	Goldings hops	(30 + 15 + 10) gm.
3, 6	(6 + 2) oz.	Soft dark brown sugar	(200 + 50) gm.
5	2 oz.	Brewers yeast	60 gm.
5	½ oz.	Gelatine	15 gm.

Brewing Stages

1. Raise the temperature of the water up to 60°C and stir in the crushed malt and flakes. Stirring continuously, raise the mash temperature up to 66°C. Leave for 1½ hours, occasionally returning the temperature back to this value.
2. Contain the mashed grain in a large grain bag to retrieve the sweet wort. Using slightly hotter water than the mash, rinse the grains to collect 4 gallons (20 litres) of extract.
3. Boil the extract with the Fuggles hops and the first quota of Goldings hops for 1½ hours. Dissolve the main batch of sugars in a little hot water and add this during the boil. Also pitch in the Irish Moss as directed on the instructions.
4. Switch off the heat, stir in the second batch of Goldings and allow them to soak for 15 minutes. Strain off the clear wort into a fermenting bin and top up to the final quantity with cold water.
5. When cool to room temperature add the yeast. Ferment 4–5 days until the specific gravity falls to 1015 and rack into gallon jars or a five gallon fermenter with an airlock. Apportion Gelatine finings and the rest of the dry hops before fitting airlocks.
6. Leave for 7 days before racking the beer from the sediment into a primed pressure barrel. Allow 7 days conditioning before sampling.

WEBSTERS (COURAGE) Halifax

YORKSHIRE BITTER

Highly individual brew; full bodied, sweetish, yet not too malty but generously hopped.

Stage	5 gallons	Original gravity 1038	25 litres
1	5½ lb.	Crushed pale malt	2800 gm.
1	5 oz.	Crushed crystal malt	150 gm.
1	5 oz.	Crushed wheat malt	150 gm.
1	3 gallons	Water for 'bitter' brewing	15 litres
3	1 tsp.	Irish moss	5 ml.
3	1 lb.	Brewing sugar	500 gm.
3	3 oz.	Fuggles hops	100 gm.
4	½ oz.	Bramling Cross hops	15 gm.
5	2 oz.	Brewers yeast	60 gm.
5	½ oz.	Gelatine	15 gm.
6	2 oz.	Brown sugar	60 gm.

Brewing Stages

1. Raise the temperature of the water up to 60°C and stir in the crushed malts. Stirring continuously, raise the mash temperature up to 66°C. Leave for 1½ hours, occasionally returning the temperature back to this value.
2. Contain the mashed grain in a large grain bag to retrieve the sweet wort. Using slightly hotter water than the mash, rinse the grains to collect 4 gallons (20 litres) of extract.
3. Boil the extract with the Fuggles hops for 1½ hours. Dissolve the brewing sugar in a little hot water and add this during the boil. Also pitch in the Irish Moss as directed on the instructions.
4. Switch off the heat, stir in the Bramling Cross hops and allow them to soak for 15 minutes. Strain off the clear wort into a fermenting bin and top up to the final quantity with cold water.
5. When cool to room temperature add the yeast. Ferment 4–5 days until the specific gravity falls to 1010 and rack into gallon jars or a secondary fermentation vessel, fitted with an airlock. Apportion Gelatine finings before fitting airlocks.
6. Leave for 7 days before racking the beer from the sediment into a primed pressure barrel. Allow 7 days conditioning before sampling.

WHITBREADS (Made by Gale's of Horndean)
POMPEY ROYAL

Ex Brickwoods Best Bitter; this robust brew is good value for money since you can still taste the hops hours after supping it—and there is not many brews that can boast such a strength of flavour.

Stage	5 gallons	Original gravity 1047	25 litres
1	5½ lb.	Crushed pale malt	2800 gm.
1	8 oz.	Crushed crystal malt	250 gm.
1	3 gallons	Water for 'bitter' brewing	15 litres
3	1 tsp.	Irish moss	5 ml.
3	1 lb.	Barley syrup	500 gm.
3	1 lb.	Soft dark brown sugar	500 gm.
3	2 oz.	Fuggles hops	60 gm.
3	1 oz.	Bramling cross hops	30 gm.
3, 4	(½ + ½) oz.	Goldings hops	(15 + 15) gm.
5	2 oz.	Brewers yeast	60 gm.
5	½ oz.	Gelatine	15 gm.
6	2 oz.	Brown sugar	60 gm.

Brewing Stages

1. Raise the temperature of the water up to 60°C and stir in the crushed malts. Stirring continuously, raise the mash temperature up to 66°C. Leave for 1½ hours, occasionally returning the temperature back to this value.
2. Contain the mashed grain in a large grain bag to retrieve the sweet wort. Using slightly hotter water than the mash, rinse the grains to collect 4 gallons (20 litres) of extract.
3. Boil the extract with the Fuggles and Bramling Cross hops and the first quota of Goldings hops for 1½ hours. Dissolve the main batch of sugar and syrup in a little hot water and add this during the boil. Also pitch in the Irish Moss as directed on the instructions.
4. Switch off the heat, stir in the second batch of Goldings and allow them to soak for 15 minutes. Strain off the clear wort into a fermenting bin and top up to the final quantity with cold water.
5. When cool to room temperature add the yeast. Ferment 4–5 days until the specific gravity falls to 1012 and rack into gallon jars or a five gallon fermenter with an airlock. Apportion gelatine finings before fitting airlocks.
6. Leave for 7 days before racking the beer from the sediment into a primed pressure barrel. Allow 7 days conditioning before sampling.

WHITBREAD (Flowers, Cheltenham)
TROPHY

Trophy is a 'generic' term for many of the best bitters under the Whitbread banner and my favourite, the Romsey version is particularly good. I have supped more pints of this brew than any other commercial beer. (NB: Romsey Brewery now closed.)

Stage	5 gallons	Original gravity 1037	25 litres
1	4 lb.	Crushed pale malt	2000 gm.
1	5 oz.	Flaked barley	150 gm.
1	2½ gallons	Water for 'bitter' brewing	12 litres
3	1 tsp.	Irish moss	5 ml.
3	1 lb.	Barley syrup	500 gm.
3	1 lb.	Soft dark brown sugar	500 gm.
3	2 oz.	Fuggles hops	60 gm.
3, 4,5	(1 + ¼ + ¼) oz.	Goldings hops	(30 + 10 + 10) gm.
5	2 oz.	Brewers yeast	60 gm.
5	½ oz.	Gelatine	15 gm.
6	2 oz.	Brown sugar	60 gm.

Brewing Stages

1. Raise the temperature of the water up to 60°C and stir in the crushed malt and grain. Stirring continuously, raise the mash temperature up to 66°C. Leave for 1½ hours, occasionally returning the temperature back to this value.

2. Contain the mashed grain in a large grain bag to retrieve the sweet wort. Using slightly hotter water than the mash, rinse the grains to collect 4 gallons (20 litres) of extract.

3. Boil the extract with the Fuggles hops and the first quota of Goldings hops for 1½ hours. Dissolve the main batch of sugar and barley syrup in a little hot water and add this during the boil. Also pitch in the Irish Moss as directed on the instructions.

4. Switch off the heat, stir in the second batch of Goldings and allow them to soak for 15 minutes. Strain off the clear wort into a fermenting bin and top up to the final quantity with cold water.

5. When cool to room temperature add the yeast. Ferment 4–5 days until the specific gravity falls to 1010 and rack into gallon jars or a secondary fermentation vessel, fitted with an airlock. Apportion Gelatine finings and the rest of the dry hops before fitting airlocks.

6. Leave for 7 days before racking the beer from the sediment into a primed pressure barrel. Allow 7 days conditioning before sampling.

YOUNGS Wandsworth
SPECIAL BITTER

A strong hoppy bitter with a distinctive taste. Maybe it is the yeast that adds to the flavour because Youngs Special is hard to come by locally and it always seemed to be served slightly cloudy. Eventually I supped some which was crystal clear and it was even better.

Stage	5 gallons	Original gravity 1047	25 litres
1	7½ lb.	Crushed pale malt	3750 gm.
1	5 oz.	Crushed crystal malt	150 gm.
1	3 gallons	Water for 'bitter' brewing	15 litres
3	1 tsp.	Irish moss	5 ml.
3	2 oz.	Fuggles hops	60 gm.
3, 4, 5	(1¼ + ½ + ¼) oz.	Goldings hops	(40 + 15 + 10) gm.
3, 6	(12 + 2) oz.	Demerara sugar	(400 + 60) gm.
5	2 oz.	Brewers yeast	60 gm.
5	¼ oz.	Gelatine	15 gm.

Brewing Stages

1. Raise the temperature of the water up to 60°C and stir in the crushed malts. Stirring continuously, raise the mash temperature up to 66°C. Leave for 1½ hours, occasionally returning the temperature back to this value.
2. Contain the mashed grain in a large grain bag to retrieve the sweet wort. Using slightly hotter water than the mash, rinse the grains to collect 4 gallons (20 litres) of extract.
3. Boil the extract with the Fuggles hops and the first quota of Goldings hops for 1½ hours. Dissolve the main batch of sugar in a little hot water and add this during the boil. Also pitch in the Irish Moss as directed on the instructions.
4. Switch off the heat, stir in the second batch of Goldings and allow them to soak for 15 minutes. Strain off the clear wort into a fermenting bin and top up to the final quantity with cold water.
5. When cool to room temperature add the yeast. Ferment 4–5 days until the specific gravity falls to 1012 and rack into gallon jars or a five gallon fermenter with an airlock. Apportion Gelatine finings and the rest of the dry hops before fitting airlocks.
6. Leave for 7 days before racking the beer from the sediment into a primed pressure barrel. Allow 7 days conditioning before sampling.

120

KEG BEERS

CHAPTER 7

BASS

WORTHINGTON 'E'

Full malty keg bitter with a very strong flavour of hops.

Stage	5 gallons	4% Alcohol	25 litres
1	4 lb.	Malt extract syrup	2000 gm.
1	8 oz.	Crushed crystal malt	250 gm.
1	1½ lb.	Soft brown sugar	750 gm.
1	2 oz.	Fuggles hops	60 gm.
1	2 gallons	Water for 'bitter' brewing	10 litres
2	2 oz. (equiv.)	Hop extract	60 gm. (equiv.)
2	1 oz.	Home brew beer yeast	30 gm.
2	½ oz.	Gelatine	15 gm.
3	2 oz.	White sugar	60 gm.

Brewing Stages

1. Boil the malt extract, crushed malt and Fuggles hops in water for 45 minutes. Carefully strain off the wort from the hops and malt grains into a fermenting bin. Rinse the spent grains and hops with two kettlefuls of hot water. Dissolve the brown sugar in hot water and add this to the bin. Top up to the final quantity with cold water.

2. When cool to room temperature pitch in the yeast and hop extract. Ferment 4–5 days until the activity abates. Rack off into secondary fermentation vessels and keep under airlock protection for another 3 days. Apportion gelatine finings and keep the beer under airlock protection for another 7 days.

3. Rack the beer off the sediment into a primed beer barrel. Allow 7 days conditioning before sampling.

COURAGE

DRAUGHT JOHN COURAGE

Draught version of the bottled strong bitter. Smooth, sweetish mellow brew with a smack of hops.

Stage	5 gallons	Original gravity 1045	25 litres
1	6½ lb.	Crushed pale malt	3250 gm.
1	8 oz.	Torrefied barley	250 gm.
1	4 oz.	Crushed crystal malt	125 gm.
1	3 gallons	Water for 'bitter' brewing	15 litres
3	1 tsp.	Irish moss	5 ml.
3	1 lb.	Light soft brown sugar	500 gm.
3	3 oz.	Goldings hops	100 gm.
3	½ oz.	Northern brewer hops	15 gm.
5	2 oz.	Brewers yeast	60 gm.
5	½ oz.	Gelatine	15 gm.
6	2 oz.	Brown sugar	60 gm.

Brewing Stages

1. Raise the temperature of the water up to 60°C and stir in the crushed malts and grain. Stirring continuously, raise the mash temperature up to 66°C. Leave for 1½ hours, occasionally returning the temperature back to this value.

2. Contain the mashed grain in a large grain bag to retrieve the sweet wort. Using slightly hotter water than the mash, rinse the grains to collect 4 gallons (20 litres) of extract.

3. Boil the extract with the hops for 1½ hours. Dissolve the main batch of sugar in a little hot water and add this during the boil. Also pitch in the Irish Moss as directed on the instructions.

4. Switch off the heat, strain off the clear wort into a fermenting bin and top up to the final quantity with cold water.

5. When cool to room temperature add the yeast. Ferment 4–5 days until the specific gravity falls to 1012 and rack into gallon jars or a secondary fermentation vessel, fitted with an airlock. Apportion Gelatine finings before fitting airlocks.

6. Leave for 7 days before racking the beer from the sediment into a primed pressure barrel. Allow 7 days conditioning before sampling.

COURAGE

TAVERN KEG

Remarkable palate fullness, malty and heavy with just enough hops.

Stage	5 gallons	Original gravity 1039	25 litres
1	3 lb.	D.M.S. malt extract	1500 gm.
1	8 oz.	Flaked barley	250 gm.
1	8 oz.	Crushed crystal malt	250 gm.
1	1 lb. 14 oz.	Light soft brown sugar	950 gm.
1	2 oz.	Fuggles hops	60 gm.
1	1 oz. (equiv.)	Hop extract	30 gm. (equiv.)
1	2½ gallons	Water for 'bitter' brewing	12 litres
2	1 oz.	Home brewers beer yeast	30 gm.
2	½ oz.	Gelatine	15 gm.
3	2 oz.	Light soft brown sugar	60 gm.

Brewing Stages

1. Stir in the malt extract, Fuggles hops and grains in luke-warm water. Slowly raise to boiling point over 30 minutes, then boil for 45 minutes. Carefully strain off the wort from the hops and malt grains into a fermenting bin. Rinse the spent grains and hops with two kettlefuls of hot water. Dissolve the main batch of sugar in hot water and add this to the bin. Top up to the final quantity with cold water.

2. When cool to room temperature pitch in the yeast. Ferment 4–5 days until the activity abates. Rack off into secondary fermentation vessels and keep under airlock protection for another 3 days. Apportion gelatine finings and keep the beer under airlock protection for another 5 days.

3. Rack the beer off the sediment into a primed beer barrel. Allow 3 days conditioning before sampling.

IND COOPE

DOUBLE DIAMOND

Popular keg bitter reputed to 'work wonders' for its loyal following. Until starting on this book I could not recollect how it tasted. Now that I have supped and brewed some it rates as one of the best keg bitters.

Stage	5 gallons	Original gravity 1038	25 litres
1	5½ lb.	Crushed pale malt	2800 gm.
1	2½ gallons	Water for 'bitter' brewing	12 litres
3	1 lb.	Barley syrup	500 gm.
3	5	Saccharin tablets	5
3	2 oz.	Fuggles hops	60 gm.
3	1 tsp.	Irish moss	5 ml.
3, 6	(6 + 2) oz.	Soft dark brown sugar	(200 + 60) gm.
5	2 oz. (equiv.)	Hop extract	60 gm. (equiv.)
5	2 oz.	Brewers yeast	60 gm.
5	½ oz.	Gelatine	15 gm.

Brewing Stages

1. Raise the temperature of the water up to 60°C and stir in the crushed malt. Stirring continuously, raise the mash temperature up to 66°C. Leave for 1½ hours, occasionally returning the temperature back to this value.
2. Contain the mashed grain in a large grain bag to retrieve the sweet wort. Using slightly hotter water than the mash, rinse the grains to collect 4 gallons (20 litres) of extract.
3. Boil the extract with the Fuggles hops for 1½ hours. Dissolve the main batch of sugar, saccharins and syrup in a little hot water and add this during the boil. Also pitch in the Irish Moss as directed on the instructions.
4. Switch off the heat, strain off the clear wort into a fermenting bin and top up to the final quantity with cold water.
5. When cool to room temperature add the yeast and hop extract. Ferment 4—5 days until the specific gravity falls to 1010 and rack into gallon jars or a five gallon fermenter with an airlock. Apportion Gelatine finings before fitting airlocks.
6. Leave for 7 days before racking the beer from the sediment into a primed pressure barrel. Allow 7 days conditioning before sampling.

JOHN SMITHS Tadcaster

YORKSHIRE BITTER

Pleasant keg bitter with a good head retention and nice amber colour. Satisfying hop flavour.

Stage	5 gallons	Original gravity 1037	25 litres
1	3 lb.	Crushed pale malt	1500 gm.
1	2 oz.	Crushed wheat malt	60 gm.
1	2 gallons	Water for 'bitter' brewing	10 litres
3	1 tsp.	Irish moss	5 ml.
3	2 lb.	Edme D.M.S. malt extract	1000 gm.
3	1 oz.	Bramling Cross hops	30 gm.
3, 4	$(1\frac{1}{2} + \frac{1}{2})$ oz.	Goldings hops	$(45 + 10)$ gm.
3, 6	$(14 + 2)$ oz.	Soft dark brown sugar	$(450 + 50)$ gm.
5	2 oz.	Brewers yeast	60 gm.
5	$\frac{1}{2}$ oz.	Gelatine	15 gm.

Brewing Stages

1. Raise the temperature of the water up to 60°C and stir in the crushed malts. Stirring continuously, raise the temperature up to 66°C. Leave for $1\frac{1}{2}$ hours, occasionally returning the temperature back to this value.
2. Contain the mashed grain in a large grain bag to retrieve the sweet wort. Using slightly hotter water than the mash, rinse the grains to collect 3 gallons (15 litres) of extract.
3. Boil the extract with the Bramling Cross hops and the first quota of Goldings hops for $1\frac{1}{2}$ hours. Dissolve the main batch of sugar and malt extract in hot water and add this during the boil. Also pitch in the Irish Moss as directed on the instructions.
4. Switch off the heat, stir in the second batch of Goldings and allow them to soak for 15 minutes. Strain off the clear wort into a fermenting bin and top up to the final quantity with cold water.
5. When cool to room temperature add the yeast. Ferment 4—5 days until the specific gravity falls to 1010 and rack into gallon jars or a secondary fermentation vessel, fitted with an airlock. Apportion Gelatine finings before fitting airlocks.
6. Leave for 7 days before racking the beer from the sediment into a primed pressure barrel. Allow 7 days conditioning before sampling.

TRUMANS

BEN TRUMANS EXPORT

Popular keg beer with a nice yeasty sweet bouquet.

Stage	5 gallons	Original gravity 1036	25 litres
1	4 lb.	Crushed pale malt	2000 gm.
1	4 oz.	Crushed wheat malt	125 gm.
1	1 lb.	Flaked maize	500 gm.
1	2½ gallons	Water for 'bitter' brewing	12 litres
3	1 tsp.	Irish moss	5 ml.
3	1 lb.	Light soft brown sugar	500 gm.
3	2 oz.	Fuggles hops	60 gm.
5	1 oz. (equiv.)	Hop extract	30 gm. (equiv.)
5	2 oz.	Brewers yeast	60 gm.
5	½ oz.	Gelatine	15 gm.
6	2 oz.	White sugar	60 gm.

Brewing Stages

1. Raise the temperature of the water up to 60°C and stir in the crushed malts and flakes. Stirring continuously, raise the mash temperature up to 66°C. Leave for 1½ hours, occasionally returning the temperature back to this value.

2. Contain the mashed grain in a large grain bag to retrieve the sweet wort. Using slightly hotter water than the mash, rinse the grains to collect 4 gallons (20 litres) of extract.

3. Boil the extract with the Fuggles hops for 1½ hours. Dissolve the main batch of sugar in a little hot water and add this during the boil. Also pitch in the Irish Moss as directed on the instructions.

4. Switch off the heat, strain off the clear wort into a fermenting bin and top up to the final quantity with cold water.

5. When cool to room temperature add the yeast and hop extract. Ferment 4–5 days until the specific gravity falls to 1010 and rack into gallon jars or a five gallon fermenter with an airlock. Apportion Gelatine finings before fitting airlocks.

6. Leave for 7 days before racking the beer from the sediment into a primed pressure barrel. Allow 7 days conditioning before sampling.

WATNEY MANN

SPECIAL BITTER

Best selling keg bitter.

Stage	5 gallons	3.5% Alcohol	25 litres
1	2 lb.	Malt extract syrup	1000 gm.
1	4 oz.	Crushed crystal malt	125 gm.
1	8 oz.	Brewing sugar	250 gm.
1	2 lb.	Demerara sugar	1000 gm.
1	1 oz.	Fuggles hops	30 gm.
1	2½ gallons	Water for 'bitter' brewing	12 litres
1	1 tsp.	Irish moss	5 ml.
2	½ oz.	Gelatine	15 gm.
2	1 oz.	Home brew beer yeast	30 gm.
2	1 oz. (equiv.)	Hop extract	30 gm. (equiv.)
2	4	Saccharin tablets	4
3	2 oz.	White sugar	60 gm.

Brewing Stages

1. Boil the malt extract, Irish Moss and crystal malt in water for 45 minutes. Carefully strain off the wort from the hops and malt grains into a fermenting bin. Rinse the spent grains and hops with two kettlefuls of hot water. Dissolve the brewing sugar and sugar in hot water and add this to the bin. Top up to the final quantity with cold water.

2. When cool to room temperature pitch in the yeast, saccharin tablets and hop extract. Ferment 4–5 days until the activity abates. Rack off into secondary fermentation vessels and keep under airlock protection for another 7 days. Apportion gelatine finings and keep the beer under airlock protection for another 7 days.

3. Rack the beer off the sediment into a primed beer barrel. Allow 3 days conditioning before sampling.

WATNEY MANN

STARLIGHT BITTER

Well balanced light gravity keg bitter.

Stage	5 gallons	Original gravity 1032	25 litres
1	4 lb.	Crushed pale malt	2000 gm.
1	8 oz.	Flaked maize	250 gm.
1	4 oz.	Flaked barley	125 gm.
1	2½ gallons	Water for 'bitter' brewing	12 litres
3	1 tsp.	Irish moss	5 ml.
3	1 lb.	Brewing sugar	500 gm.
3	1 oz.	Fuggles hops	30 gm.
5	1 oz. (equiv.)	Hop extract	30 gm. (equiv.)
5	2 oz.	Brewers yeast	60 gm.
5	½ oz.	Gelatine	15 gm.
6	2 oz.	White sugar	60 gm.

Brewing Stages

1. Raise the temperature of the water up to 60°C and stir in the crushed malt, flakes and grain. Stirring continuously, raise the mash temperature up to 66°C. Leave for 1½ hours, occasionally returning the temperature back to this value.
2. Contain the mashed grain in a large grain bag to retrieve the sweet wort. Using slightly hotter water than the mash, rinse the grains to collect 4 gallons (20 litres) of extract.
3. Boil the extract with the Fuggles hops for 1½ hours. Dissolve the brewing sugar in a little hot water and add this during the boil. Also pitch in the Irish Moss as directed on the instructions.
4. Strain off the clear wort into a fermenting bin and top up to the final quantity with cold water.
5. When cool to room temperature add the yeast and hop extract. Ferment 4−5 days until the specific gravity falls to 1010 and rack into gallon jars or a secondary fermentation vessel, fitted with an airlock. Apportion Gelatine finings before fitting airlocks.
6. Leave for 7 days before racking the beer from the sediment into a primed pressure barrel. Allow 3 days conditioning before sampling.

WATNEY MANN

SPECIAL MILD

Watney always had a good name for brewing dark beers and this popular brew was better than the majority of mild ales I sampled. Judging by the number of people that drank it, others felt the same way.

Stage	5 gallons	Original gravity 1031	25 litres
1	4¼ lb.	Crushed pale malt	2200 gm.
1	4 oz.	Flaked barley	125 gm.
1	2½ gallons	Water for 'mild ale' brewing	10 litres
3	1 lb.	Soft dark brown sugar	500 gm.
3	2 oz.	Black treacle	60 gm.
3	1 oz.	Fuggles hops	30 gm.
5	5	Saccharin tablets	5
5	1½ oz. (equiv.)	Hop extract	50 gm. (equiv.)
5	2 oz.	Brewers yeast	60 gm.
5	½ oz.	Gelatine	15 gm.
6	2 oz.	Brown sugar	60 gm.

Brewing Stages

1. Raise the temperature of the water up to 60°C and stir in the crushed malts. Stirring continuously, raise the mash temperature up to 66°C. Leave for 1½ hours, occasionally returning the temperature back to this value.

2. Contain the mashed grain in a large grain bag to retrieve the sweet wort. Using slightly hotter water than the mash, rinse the grains to collect 4 gallons (20 litres) of extract.

3. Boil the extract with the Fuggles hops for 1½ hours. Dissolve the main batch of sugar and black treacle in a little hot water and add this during the boil.

4. Switch off the heat, strain off the clear wort into a fermenting bin and top up to the final quantity with cold water.

5. When cool to room temperature add the yeast, hop extract and saccharin tablets. Ferment 4—5 days until the specific gravity falls to 1010 and rack into gallon jars or a five gallon fermenter with an airlock. Apportion gelatine finings before fitting airlocks.

6. Leave for 7 days before racking the beer from the sediment into a primed pressure barrel. Allow 5 days conditioning before sampling.

WHITBREAD

TANKARD

Full bodied keg bitter with well balanced smooth flavour.

Stage	5 gallons	Original gravity 1039	25 litres
1	4½ lb.	Crushed pale malt	2250 gm.
1	4 oz.	Crushed torrefied barley	125 gm.
1	3 gallons	Water for 'bitter' brewing	15 litres
3	1 lb.	Barley syrup	500 gm.
3	1 tsp.	Irish moss	5 ml.
3	2 oz.	Fuggles hops	60 gm.
3, 4	(1 + ½) oz.	Bramling Cross hops	(30 + 15) gm.
3, 6	(14 + 2) oz.	Demerara sugar	(450 + 50) gm.
5	2 oz.	Brewers yeast	60 gm.
5	½ oz.	Gelatine	15 gm.

Brewing Stages

1. Raise the temperature of the water up to 60°C and stir in the crushed malt and grain. Stirring continuously, raise the mash temperature up to 66°C. Leave for 1½ hours, occasionally returning the temperature back to this value.
2. Contain the mashed grain in a large bag to retrieve the sweet wort. Using slightly hotter water than the mash, rinse the grains to collect 4 gallons (20 litres) of extract.
3. Boil the extract with the Fuggles hops and the first quota of Bramling Cross hops for 1½ hours. Dissolve the main batch of sugar in a little hot water and add this during the boil. Also pitch in the Irish Moss as directed on the instructions.
4. Switch off the heat, stir in the second batch of Bramling Cross hops and allow them to soak for 15 minutes. Strain off the clear wort into a fermenting bin and top up to the final quantity with cold water.
5. When cool to room temperature add the yeast. Ferment 4–5 days until the specific gravity falls to 1010 and rack into gallon jars or a secondary fermentation vessel, fitted with an airlock. Apportion gelatine finings before fitting airlocks.
6. Leave for 7 days before racking the beer from the sediment into a primed pressure barrel. Allow 7 days conditioning before sampling.

YOUNGER Edinburgh

TARTAN KEG

A predominant hop flavour is the main characteristic of this malty keg bitter. A relatively low carbonation makes it a smooth drink.

Stage	5 gallons	Original gravity 1036	25 litres
1	4½ lb.	Crushed pale malt	2250 gm.
1	4 oz.	Crushed flaked barley	125 gm.
1	2½ gallons	Water for 'pale ale' brewing	12 litres
3	1 tsp.	Irish moss	5 ml.
3	1 lb.	Malt extract syrup	500 gm.
3	½ lb.	Soft dark brown sugar	250 gm.
3	2 oz.	Fuggles hops	60 gm.
3	1½ oz.	Northern Brewer hops	45 gm.
5	2 oz.	Brewers yeast	60 gm.
5	½ oz.	Gelatine	15 gm.
6	2 oz.	White sugar	60 gm.

Brewing Stages

1. Raise the temperature of the water up to 60°C and stir in the crushed malts. Stirring continuously, raise the mash temperature up to 66°C. Leave for 1½ hours, occasionally returning the temperature back to this value.
2. Contain the mashed grain in a large grain bag to retrieve the sweet wort. Using slightly hotter water than the mash, rinse the grains to collect 4 gallons (20 litres) of extract.
3. Boil the extract with the hops for 1½ hours. Dissolve the malt extract syrup and the main batch of sugar in a little hot water and add this during the boil. Also pitch in the Irish Moss as directed on the instructions.
4. Switch off the heat, strain off the clear wort into a fermenting bin and top up to the final quantity with cold water.
5. When cool to room temperature add the yeast. Ferment 4—5 days until the specific gravity falls to 1010 and rack into gallon jars or a five gallon fermenter with an airlock. Apportion gelatine finings before fitting airlocks.
6. Leave for 7 days before racking the beer from the sediment into a primed pressure barrel. Allow 7 days conditioning before sampling.

BEERS
OF THE
WORLD

AMERICA
BUDWEISER Lager Beer

'The largest selling beer in the world' claim the brewers, Anheuser-Busch Incorporated. The label on the can commanded as much interest from me as the beer itself.

'This is the famous Budweiser beer. We know of no brand produced by any other brewer which costs so much to brew and age. Our exclusive Beechwood Ageing produces a taste, a smoothness and a drinkability you will find in no other beer at any price. "King of Beers"—genuine, brewed in the UK.'

Try it for yourself—it *is* good!

Stage	5 gallons	Original gravity 1046	25 litres
1	7 lb.	Crushed lager malt	3500 gm.
1	1 lb. 10 oz.	Flaked rice	800 gm.
1	3 gallons	Water for 'lager' brewing	15 litres
3	1 tsp.	Irish moss	5 ml.
3	2 oz.	Hallertau hops	60 gm.
5	2 oz.	Lager yeast	60 gm.
5	½ oz.	Gelatine	15 gm.
6	¼ tsp./pint	White sugar	5 ml./litre

Brewing Stages

1. Raise the temperature of the water up to 40°C and stir in the crushed malt and flakes. Stirring continuously, raise the mash temperature up to 50°C. Let it stand for half an hour and then raise the temperature again up to 66°C. Leave for 1½ hours, occasionally returning the temperature back to this value.

2. Contain the mashed grain in a large grain bag to retrieve the sweet wort. Using slightly hotter water than the mash, rinse the grains to collect 4 gallons (20 litres) of extract.

3. Boil the extract with the hops for 1½ hours. Also pitch in the Irish Moss as directed on the instructions.

4. Switch off the heat and strain off the clear wort into a fermenting bin and top up to the final quantity with cold water.

5. When cool to room temperature add the yeast. Ferment until the specific gravity falls to 1012 and rack into gallon jars or a five gallon fermenter with an airlock. Apportion Gelatine finings before fitting airlocks.

6. Leave for 7 days before racking the beer from the sediment into primed beer bottles. Allow 21 days conditioning before sampling.

AMERICA

COLD 45 Strong Export Lager

Malt liquor brewed by the National Brewery Company and in this country by Courages under licence to the original recipe.

Stage	5 gallons	Original gravity 1047	25 litres
1	7 lb.	Crushed lager malt	3500 gm.
1	5 oz.	Crushed crystal malt	150 gm.
1	1 lb. 10 oz.	Flaked maize	800 gm.
1	3 gallons	Water for 'lager' brewing	15 litres
3	1 tsp.	Irish moss	5 ml.
3	2 oz.	Hallertau hops	60 gm.
5	2 oz.	Lager yeast	60 gm.
5	½ oz.	Gelatine	15 gm.
5	1 tsp.	Citric acid	5 ml.
6	¼ tsp./pint	White sugar	5 ml./litre

Brewing Stages

1. Raise the temperature of the water up to 55°C and stir in the crushed malts and flakes. Stirring continuously, raise the mash temperature up to 66°C. Leave for 1½ hours, occasionally returning the temperature back to this value.

2. Contain the mashed grain in a large grain bag to retrieve the sweet wort. Using slightly hotter water than the mash, rinse the grains to collect 4 gallons (20 litres) of extract.

3. Boil the extract with the Hallertau hops for 1½ hours. Also pitch in the Irish Moss as directed on the instructions.

4. Switch off the heat, strain off the clear wort into a fermenting bin and top up to the final quantity with cold water.

5. When cool to room temperature add the yeast and citric acid. Ferment until the specific gravity falls to 1012 and rack into gallon jars or a secondary fermentation vessel, fitted with an airlock. Apportion gelatine finings before fitting airlocks.

6. Leave for 7 days racking the beer from the sediment into primed beer bottles. Allow 21 days conditioning before sampling.

AMERICA

SCHLITZ

'The beer that made Milwaukee famous'. Extremely pale and delicate beer. Served chilled it is a gorgeous beer for a hot summer day. Also it is an excellent accompaniment for meals.

Stage	5 gallons	Original gravity 1048	25 litres
1	8 lb.	Crushed lager malt	4000 gm.
1	12 oz.	Flaked maize	400 gm.
1	3 gallons	Water for 'lager' brewing	15 litres
3	1 tsp.	Irish moss	5 ml.
3	1 oz.	Hallertau hops	30 gm.
5	2 oz.	Lager yeast	60 gm.
5	½ oz.	Gelatine	15 gm.
6	½ tsp./pint	White sugar	5 ml./litre

Brewing Stages

1. Raise the temperature of the water up to 45°C and stir in the crushed malt and flakes. Stirring continuously, raise the mash temperature up to 55°C. Let it stand for half an hour and then raise the temperature again up to 66°C. Leave for 1½ hours, occasionally returning the temperature back to this value.
2. Contain the mashed grain in a large grain bag to retrieve the sweet wort. Using slightly hotter water than the mash, rinse the grains to collect 4 gallons (20 litres) of extract.
3. Boil the extract with the hops for 1½ hours. Pitch in the Irish Moss as directed on the instructions.
4. Switch off the heat, strain off the clear wort into a fermenting bin and top up to the final quantity with cold water.
5. When cool to room temperature add the yeast. Ferment in a cool place until the specific gravity falls to 1015 and rack into gallon jars or a five gallon fermenter with an airlock. Apportion Gelatine finings before fitting airlocks.
6. Leave for 21 days before racking the beer from the sediment into primed beer bottles. Allow 21 days maturation before sampling.

AUSTRALIA

CASTLEMAINE XXXX BITTER

Not like a traditional English bitter beer but more of a 'hoppy' lager. Nevertheless, a very palatable and refreshing brew.

Stage	5 gallons	Original gravity 1044	25 litres
1	5¾ lb.	Crushed pale malt	2900 gm.
1	1 lb.	Flaked maize	500 gm.
1	3 gallons	Water for 'lager' brewing	15 litres
3	1 tsp.	Irish moss	5 ml.
3	1 lb.	Brewing sugar	500 gm.
3	2¾ oz.	Hallertau hops	80 gm.
5	2 oz.	Lager yeast	60 gm.
5	½ oz.	Gelatine	15 gm.
6	½ tsp./pint	White sugar	5 ml./litre

Brewing Stages
1. Raise the temperature of the water up to 55°C and stir in the crushed malt and flakes. Stirring continuously, raise the mash temperature up to 66°C. Leave for 1½ hours, occasionally returning the temperature back to this value.
2. Contain the mashed grain in a large grain bag to retrieve the sweet wort. Using slightly hotter water than the mash, rinse the grains to collect 4 gallons (20 litres) of extract.
3. Boil the extract with the hops for 1½ hours. Dissolve the brewing sugar in a little water and add this during the boil. Also pitch in the Irish Moss as directed on the instructions.
4. Switch off the heat, strain off the clear wort into a fermenting bin and top up to the final quantity with cold water.
5. When cool to room temperature add the yeast. Ferment 4–5 days until the specific gravity falls to 1012 and rack into gallon jars or a secondary fermentation vessel, fitted with an airlock. Apportion Gelatine finings before fitting airlocks.
6. Leave for 7 days before racking the beer from the sediment into primed beer bottles. Allow 7 days maturation before sampling.

AUSTRALIA

FOSTERS LAGER

Cricket, Kangaroos and cans of Fosters Lager *are* Australia to us 'Pommies'. This famous brew has a delicate flavour with a beery bouquet. Serve well chilled.

Stage	5 gallons	Original gravity 1046	25 litres
1	6½ lb.	Crushed lager malt	3250 gm.
1	1 lb.	Flaked rice	500 gm.
1	3 gallons	Water for 'lager' brewing	15 litres
3	1 tsp.	Irish moss	5 ml.
3	12 oz.	Brewing sugar	400 gm.
3	1½ oz.	Hallertau hops	45 gm.
5	2 oz.	Lager yeast	60 gm.
5	½ oz.	Gelatine	15 gm.
6	½ tsp./pint	White sugar	5 ml./litre

Brewing Stages

1. Raise the temperature of the water up to 45°C and stir in the crushed malt and flakes. Stirring continuously, raise the mash temperature up to 55°C. Let it stand for half an hour and then raise the temperature again up to 66°C. Leave for 1½ hours, occasionally returning the temperature back to this value.
2. Contain the mashed grain in a large grain bag to retrieve the sweet wort. Using slightly hotter water than the mash, rinse the grains to collect 4 gallons (20 litres) of extract.
3. Boil the extract with the hops for 1½ hours. Dissolve the brewing sugar in a little hot water and add this during the boil. Also pitch in the Irish Moss as directed on the instructions.
4. Switch off the heat, strain off the clear wort into a fermenting bin and top up to the final quantity with cold water.
5. When cool to room temperature add the yeast. Ferment in a cool place until the specific gravity falls to 1012 and rack into gallon jars or a secondary fermentation vessel, fitted with an airlock. Apportion gelatine finings before fitting airlocks.
6. Leave for 14 days before racking the beer from the sediment into primed beer bottles. Allow 21 days maturation before sampling.

AUSTRALIA

RESCHS PILSNER

Brewed and canned by Tooths, this lager has ample strength and flavour despite the relatively low hop rate.

Stage	5 gallons	Original gravity 1043	25 litres
1	5 lb.	Crushed lager malt	2500 gm.
1	¼ lb.	Flaked maize	250 gm.
1	3 gallons	Water for 'lager' brewing	15 litres
3	1 tsp.	Irish moss	5 ml.
3	2 lb.	Golden syrup	1000 gm.
3	1½ oz.	Hallertau hops	50 gm.
5	2 oz.	Lager yeast	60 gm.
5	½ oz.	Gelatine	15 gm.
6	2 oz.	White sugar	60 gm.

Brewing Stages

1. Raise the temperature of the water up to 45°C and stir in the crushed malt and flakes. Stirring continuously, raise the mash temperature up to 55°C. Let it stand for half an hour and then raise the temperature again up to 66°C. Leave for 1½ hours, occasionally returning the temperature back to this value.
2. Contain the mashed grain in a large grain bag to retrieve the sweet wort. Using slightly hotter water than the mash, rinse the grains to collect 4 gallons (20 litres) of extract.
3. Boil the extract with the hops for 1½ hours. Dissolve the syrup in a little hot water and add this during the boil. Also pitch in the Irish Moss as directed on the instructions.
4. Switch off the heat, strain off the clear wort into a fermenting bin and top up to the final quantity with cold water.
5. When cool to room temperature add the yeast. Ferment in a cool place until the specific gravity falls to 1010 and rack into gallon jars or a five gallon fermenter with an airlock. Apportion gelatine finings before fitting airlocks.
6. Leave for 21 days before racking the beer from the sediment into primed beer bottles. Allow 21 days maturation before sampling.

AUSTRALIA

SOUTHWARK BITTER

Light flavoured sweetish beer very much like a lager. Brewed by the Southern Australian Brewing Company in Adelaide.

Stage	5 gallons	Original gravity 1041	25 litres
1	5¼ lb.	Crushed pale malt	2650 gm.
1	1 lb.	Flaked maize	500 gm.
1	3 gallons	Water for 'lager' brewing	15 litres
3	1 tsp.	Irish moss	5 ml.
3	12 oz.	Brewing sugar	400 gm.
3	2½ oz.	Goldings hops	75 gm.
5	5	Saccharin tablets	5
5	2 oz.	Lager yeast	60 gm.
5	½ oz.	Gelatine	15 gm.
6	½ tsp./pint	White sugar	5 ml./litre

Brewing Stages

1. Raise the temperature of the water up to 55°C and stir in the crushed malt and flakes. Stirring continuously, raise the mash temperature up to 66°C. Leave for 1½ hours, occasionally returning the temperature back to this value.
2. Contain the mashed grain in a large grain bag to retrieve the sweet wort. Using slightly hotter water than the mash, rinse the grains to collect 4 gallons (20 litres) of extract.
3. Boil the extract with the hops for 1½ hours. Dissolve the brewing sugar in a little hot water and add this during the boil. Also pitch in the Irish Moss as directed on the instructions.
4. Switch off the heat, strain off the clear wort into a fermenting bin and top up to the final quantity with cold water.
5. When cool to room temperature add the yeast and saccharin tablets. Ferment 4–5 days until the specific gravity falls to 1012 and rack into gallon jars or a secondary fermentation vessel, fitted with an airlock. Apportion gelatine finings before fitting airlocks.
6. Leave for 7 days before racking the beer from the sediment into primed beer bottles. Allow 7 days maturation before sampling.

BELGIUM

CHIMAY

An outstanding naturally conditioned beer brewed by the Trappist monks in Chimay. They certainly know their business.

Deliciously smooth, sweet and mellow, it must rank as one of the best beers in the world. Bon Sante!

Stage	3 gallons	Original gravity 1075	15 litres
1	6½ lb.	Crushed pale malt	3250 gm.
1	1 oz.	Crushed black malt	30 gm.
1	3 gallons	Water for 'strong ale' brewing	15 litres
3	12 oz.	Soft dark brown sugar	400 gm.
3	8 oz.	Blended honey	250 gm.
3	2 oz.	Hallertau hops	60 gm.
3	1 oz.	Goldings hops	30 gm.
4	2 oz.	Brewers yeast	60 gm.
6	¼ tsp./pint	White sugar	5 ml./litre

Brewing Stages

1. Raise the temperature of the water up to 55°C and stir in the crushed malts. Stirring continuously raise the temperature up to 66°C. Leave for 1½ hours occasionally returning the temperature back to this value.
2. Contain the mashed grain in a large grain bag to retrieve the sweet wort. Using slightly hotter water than the mash slowly and gently rinse the grains to collect 3½ gallons (16 litres) of extract.
3. Boil the extract with the hops and the sugar and the honey dissolved in a little water until the volume has been reduced to just over 3 gallons (15 litres). Strain off and divide equally in four gallon jars. Fit airlocks.
4. When cool add the yeast and ferment until the vigorous activity abates. Then siphon off into three one gallon jars, filling each to the base of the neck. Refit airlocks, and check regularly to ensure they don't dry out.
5. It will take weeks to complete the fermentation, after which the beer should be racked again, taking with it a minute quantity of the yeast sediment.
6. Store for six months before bottling in primed beer bottle (preferably 'nips').
7. Mature for 18 months before sampling.

BELGIUM

STELLA ARTOIS

Strong beautifully brewed lager with a generous hop quota which rounds off the residual malt sweetness.

Stage	4 gallons	Original gravity 1050	20 litres
1	7 lb.	Crushed lager malt	3500 gm.
1	12 oz.	Crushed wheat malt	400 gm.
	3 gallons	Water for 'lager' brewing	15 litres
	1 tsp.	Irish moss	5 ml.
13	1½ oz.	Hallertau hops	45 gm.
33, 4	(1½ + ½) oz.	Saaz hops	(45 + 15) gm.
5	2 oz.	Lager yeast	60 gm.
5	½ oz.	Gelatine	15 gm.
6	½ tsp./pint	White sugar	5 ml./litre

Brewing Stages

1. Raise the temperature of the water up to 45°C and stir in the crushed malts. Stirring continuously raise the mash temperature up to 55°C. Let it stand for half an hour and then raise the temperature again up to 66°C. Leave for 1½ hours occasionally returning the temperature back to this value.
2. Contain the mashed grain in a large grain bag to retrieve the sweet wort. Using slightly hotter water than the mash, rinse the grains to collect 4 gallons (20 litres) of extract.
3. Boil the extract with the Hallertau hops and the first quota of Saaz hops for 1½ hours. Pitch in the Irish Moss as directed on the instructions.
4. Switch off the heat, stir in the second batch of Saaz hops and allow them to soak for 15 minutes. Strain off the clear wort into a fermenting bin and top up to the final quantity with cold water.
5. When cool to room temperature add the yeast. Ferment in a cool place until the specific gravity falls to 1012 and rack into gallon jars or a five gallon fermenter with an airlock. Apportion gelatine finings before fitting airlocks.
6. Leave for 21 days before racking the beer from the sediment into primed beer bottles. Allow 21 days maturation before sampling.

CZECHOSLAVAKIA

PILSNER URQUELL

Really called 'Pizenske Prazdo', it is sold here as Pilsner Urquell, and it is from this German version that the word 'Pilsner' originated. One of the finest lagers in the world with a tremendous depth of flavour from the malt and Saaz hops.

Stage	4 gallons	Original gravity 1050	20 litres
1	7 lb. 10 oz.	Crushed lager malt	3850 gm.
1	3 gallons	Water for 'lager' brewing	15 litres
3	1 tsp.	Irish moss	5 ml.
3, 4, 5	$(2\frac{1}{2} + \frac{1}{2} + \frac{1}{4})$ oz.	Saaz hops	$(75 + 15 + 10)$ gm.
5	2 oz.	Lager yeast	60 gm.
5	$\frac{1}{2}$ oz.	Gelatine	15 gm.
6	$\frac{1}{4}$ tsp./pint	White sugar	5 ml./litre

Brewing Stages

1. Raise the temperature of the water up to 45°C and stir in the crushed malt. Stirring continuously, raise the mash temperature up to 55°C. Let it stand for half an hour and then raise the temperature again up to 66°C. Leave for 1 hour, occasionally returning the temperature back to this value.
2. Contain the mashed grain in a large grain bag to retrieve the sweet wort. Using slightly hotter water than the mash, rinse the grains to collect 4 gallons (20 litres) of extract.
3. Boil the extract with the first quota of hops for 1½ hours. Pitch in the Irish Moss as directed on the instructions.
4. Switch off the heat, stir in the second batch of hops and allow them to soak for 15 minutes. Strain off the clear wort into a fermenting bin and top up to the final quantity with cold water.
5. When cool to room temperature add the yeast. Ferment in a cool place until the specific gravity falls to 1015 and rack into gallon jars or a secondary fermentation vessel, fitted with an airlock. Apportion gelatine finings and the rest of the dry hops before fitting airlocks.
6. Leave for 21 days before racking the beer from the sediment into primed beer bottles. Allow 30 days maturation before sampling.

FRANCE

KRONENBOURG Export Lager

Enjoyable lager with distinctive flavour.

Stage	5 gallons	Original gravity 1052	25 litres
1	7 lb.	Crushed lager malt	3600 gm.
1	1¼ lb.	Flaked maize	625 gm.
1	3 gallons	Water for 'lager' brewing	15 litres
3	1 tsp.	Irish moss	5 ml.
3	1 lb.	Blended honey	500 gm.
3	1 oz.	Goldings hops	30 gm.
3, 4	(1¼ + ½) oz.	Saaz hops	(40 + 10) gm.
5	2 oz.	Lager yeast	60 gm.
5	½ oz.	Gelatine	15 gm.
6	¼ tsp./pint	White sugar	5 ml./litre

Brewing Stages

1. Raise the temperature of the water up to 45°C and stir in the crushed malt and flakes. Stirring continuously, raise the mash temperature up to 55°C. Let it stand for half an hour and then raise the temperature again up to 66°C. Leave for 1½ hours, occasionally returning the temperature back to this value.
2. Contain the mashed grain in a large grain bag to retrieve the sweet wort. Using slightly hotter water than the mash, rinse the grains to collect 4 gallons (20 litres) of extract.
3. Boil the extract with the first quota of Saaz hops for 1½ hours. Dissolve the honey in a little hot water and add this during the boil. Also pitch in the Irish Moss as directed on the instructions.
4. Switch off the heat, stir in the rest of the hops and allow them to soak for 15 minutes. Strain off the clear wort into a fermenting bin and top up to the final quantity with cold water.
5. When cool to room temperature add the yeast. Ferment in a cool place until the specific gravity falls to 1015 and rack into gallon jars or a secondary fermentation vessel, fitted with an airlock. Apportion gelatine finings before fitting airlocks.
6. Leave for 30 days before racking the beer from the sediment into primed beer bottles. Allow 21 days conditioning before sampling.

GERMANY

DORTMUNDER
HANSA EXPORT

Full bodied lager, slightly sweet with sufficient hop bite.

Stage	4 gallons	Original gravity 1053	20 litres
1	8 lb.	Crushed lager malt	4000 gm.
1	3 gallons	Water for 'lager' brewing	15 litres
3	1 tsp.	Irish moss	5 ml.
3	2½ oz.	Saaz hops	75 gm.
5	2 oz.	Lager yeast	60 gm.
5	½ oz.	Gelatine	15 gm.
6	¼ tsp./pint	White sugar	5 ml./litre

Brewing Stages

1. Raise the temperature of the water up to 55°C and stir in the crushed malt. Let it stand for half an hour and then raise the temperature again up to 67°C. Leave for 1½ hours occasionally returning the temperature back to this value.

2. Contain the mashed grain in a large grain bag to retrieve the sweet wort. Using slightly hotter water than the mash, rinse the grains to collect 4 gallons (20 litres) of extract.

3. Boil the extract with the hops for 1½ hours. Pitch in the Irish Moss as directed on the instructions.

4. Switch off the heat, strain off the clear wort into a fermenting bin and top up to the final quantity with cold water.

5. When cool to room temperature add the yeast. Ferment in a cool place until the specific gravity falls to 1015 and rack into gallon jars or a five gallon fermenter with an airlock. Apportion gelatine finings before fitting airlocks.

6. Leave for 21 days before racking the beer from the sediment into primed beer bottles. Allow 30 days maturation before sampling.

GERMANY

HOLSTEN PILSNER LAGER

A true German lager brewed and bottled in the country of origin following the 'Rheinheitsgebot' principles. (See opposite page).

Stage	5 gallons	Original gravity 1046	25 litres
1	8 lb.	Crushed lager malt	4000 gm.
1	8 oz.	Crushed wheat malt	250 gm.
1	5 oz.	Crushed crystal malt	150 gm.
1	3 gallons	Water for 'lager' brewing	15 litres
3	1 tsp.	Irish moss	5 ml.
3	2¾ oz.	Hallertau hops	75 gm.
4	½ oz.	Goldings hops	20 gm.
5	2 oz.	Lager yeast	60 gm.
5	½ oz.	Gelatine	15 gm.
6	¼ tsp./pint	White sugar	5 ml./litre

Brewing Stages

1. Raise the temperature of the water up to 40°C and stir in the crushed malts. Stirring continuously, raise the mash temperature up to 50°C. Let it stand for half an hour and then raise the temperature again up to 66°C. Leave for 1½ hours, occasionally returning the temperature back to this value.
2. Contain the mashed grain in a large grain bag to retrieve the sweet wort. Using slightly hotter water than the mash, rinse the grains to collect 4 gallons (20 litres) of extract.
3. Boil the extract with the Hallertau hops for 1½ hours. Pitch in the Irish Moss as directed on the instructions.
4. Switch off the heat, stir in the batch of Goldings hops and allow them to soak for 15 minutes. Strain off the clear wort into a fermenting bin and top up to the final quantity with cold water.
5. When cool to room temperature add the yeast. Ferment in a cool place (10°C) until the specific gravity falls to 1012 and rack into gallon jars or a secondary fermentation vessel, fitted with an airlock. Apportion Gelatine finings before fitting airlocks.
6. Leave for 30 days before racking the beer from the sediment into primed beer bottles. Allow 30 days maturation before sampling.

GERMANY
LOWENBRAU Light Blonde Special

In 1516, Duke Wilhelm IV of Bavaria decreed 'Rhein-heitsgebot', or Pledge of Purity. According to this pledge only barley hops and water should be used in the brewing of beer.

This strong well matured lager is an excellent example of beer brewed to the German Beer Purity standards.

Stage	4 gallons	Original gravity 1060	20 litres
1	9 lb.	Crushed lager malt	4500 gm.
1	3 oz.	Crushed crystal malt	100 gm.
1	3 gallons	Water for 'lager' brewing	15 litres
3	1 tsp.	Irish moss	5 ml.
3	1 oz.	Hallertau hops	30 gm.
3, 4, 5	$(1\frac{1}{2} + \frac{1}{4} + \frac{1}{4})$ oz.	Saaz hops	$(45 + 10 + 10)$ gm.
5	2 oz.	Lager yeast	60 gm.
5	$\frac{1}{2}$ oz.	Gelatine	15 gm.
6	$\frac{1}{4}$ tsp./pint	White sugar	5 ml./litre

Brewing Stages

1. Raise the temperature of the water up to 45°C and stir in the crushed malts. Stirring continuously, raise the mash temperature up to 55°C. Let it stand for half an hour and then raise the temperature again up to 66°C. Leave for $1\frac{1}{2}$ hours, occasionally returning the temperature back to this value.

2. Contain the mashed grain in a large grain bag to retrieve the sweet wort. Using slightly hotter water than the mash, rinse the grains to collect 4 gallons (20 litres) of extract.

3. Boil the extract with the Hallertau hops and the first quota of Saaz hops for $1\frac{1}{2}$ hours. Pitch in the Irish Moss as directed on the instructions.

4. Switch off the heat, stir in the second batch of Saaz hops and allow them to soak for 15 minutes. Strain off the clear wort into a fermenting bin and top up to the final quantity with cold water.

5. When cool to room temperature add the yeast. Ferment in a cool place until the specific gravity falls to 1015 and rack into gallon jars or a five gallon fermenter with an airlock. Apportion Gelatine finings and the rest of the dry hops before fitting airlocks.

6. Leave for 30 days before racking the beer from the sediment into primed beer bottles. Allow 30 days maturation before sampling.

HOLLAND

GROLSCH LAGER

From the 'Bierbrouwerij' in Groenlo comes this very strong full flavoured completely natural lager

Stage	3 gallons	Original gravity 1068	15 litres
1	7¼ lb.	Crushed lager malt	3750 gm.
1	3 oz.	Crushed crystal malt	100 gm.
1	3 gallons	Water for 'lager' brewing	15 litres
3	1 tsp.	Irish moss	5 ml.
3	3 oz.	Hallertau hops	100 gm.
5	2 oz.	Lager yeast	60 gm.
5	¼ oz.	Gelatine	15 gm.
6	½ tsp./pint	White sugar	5 ml./litre

Brewing Stages

1. Raise the temperature of the water up to 45°C and stir in the crushed malts. Stirring continuously, raise the mash temperature up to 55°C. Let it stand for half an hour and then raise the temperature again up to 66°C. Leave for 1½ hours, occasionally returning the temperature back to this value.

2. Contain the mashed grain in a large grain bag to retrieve the sweet wort. Using slightly hotter water than the mash, rinse the grains to collect 4 gallons (20 litres) of extract.

3. Boil the extract with the hops for 1½ hours. Pitch in the Irish Moss as directed on the instructions.

4. Switch off the heat, strain off the clear wort into a fermenting bin and top up to the final quantity with cold water.

5. When cool to room temperature add the yeast and ferment in a cool place for five days. Then rack off into three one gallon jars. Complete the fermentation and rack into fresh jars and apportion gelatine finings before fitting airlocks again. Refit airlocks, and check regularly to ensure they don't dry out.

6. Leave for 21 days before racking the beer from the sediment into primed beer bottles. Allow 30 days maturation before sampling.

Do not leave your lager too long

One day a friend offered to give me a hand at clearing out the rubbish which had accumulated in my brewstore. In there we found two dozen bottles of strong lager which were put down to mature some months previous.

Wondering if they were still sound, I picked up the first bottle pulled off the stopper, had a mouthful and poured the rest down the sink. I picked up the second bottle, pulled off the stopper, had a mouthful and poured the rest down the sink. Pick up another bottle, pulled off the stopper had a sink and poured the rest down the mouth. Pick up another bottle, sink the stopper and pulled the mouth down the sink. Pittled anwer, stopped pulling and sink the mouth down the bottle, picked up nuvver, pulled down the sink and stopped the pullover and sank the mouth in down the bockle and pulled it out den i sank and z z z z z z z z

ITALY Naples

PERONI BIRRA

First class beer; certainly the best looking lager I have come across.

Stage	5 gallons	Original gravity 1044	25 litres
1	6½ lb.	Crushed lager malt	3250 gm.
1	4 oz.	Crushed crystal malt	125 gm.
1	1 lb. 8 oz.	Flaked rice	750 gm.
1	3 gallons	Water for 'lager' brewing	15 litres
3	1 tsp.	Irish moss	5 ml.
3, 4	(2 + 1) oz.	Saaz hops	(60 + 30) gm.
5	2 oz.	Lager yeast	60 gm.
5	½ oz.	Gelatine	15 gm.
6	¼ tsp./pint	White sugar	5 ml./litre

Brewing Stages

1. Raise the temperature of the water up to 45°C and stir in the crushed malts and flakes. Stirring continuously, raise the mash temperature up to 55°C. Let it stand for half an hour and then raise the temperature again up to 66°C. Leave for one hour, occasionally returning the temperature back to this value.
2. Contain the mashed grain in a large grain bag to retrieve the sweet wort. Using slightly hotter water than the mash, rinse the grains to collect 4 gallons (20 litres) of extract.
3. Boil the extract with the first quota of Saaz hops for 1½ hours. Pitch in the Irish Moss as directed on the instructions.
4. Switch off the heat, stir in the second batch of hops and allow them to soak for 15 minutes. Strain off the clear wort into a fermenting bin and top up to the final quantity with cold water.
5. When cool to room temperature add the yeast. Ferment in a cool place until the specific gravity falls to 1012 and rack into gallon jars or a five gallon fermenter with an airlock. Apportion gelatine finings before fitting airlocks.
6. Leave for 21 days before racking the beer from the sediment into primed beer bottles. Allow 21 days conditioning before sampling.

LUXEMBOURG

DIEKIRCH LAGER

Typical high class continental lager. Everything is right about this brew—flavour, balance, colour and strength—Most enjoyable drink.

Stage	5 gallons	Original gravity 1045	25 litres
1	8 lb.	Crushed lager malt	4000 gm.
1	3 oz.	Crushed crystal malt	100 gm.
1	3 gallons	Water for 'lager' brewing	15 litres
3	1 tsp.	Irish moss	5 ml.
3, 4	(2½ + ½) oz.	Saaz hops	(75 + 15) gm.
5	2 oz.	Lager yeast	60 gm.
5	½ oz.	Gelatine	15 gm.
6	½ tsp./pint	White sugar	5 ml./litre

Brewing Stages

1. Raise the temperature of the water up to 45°C and stir in the crushed malts. Stirring continuously, raise the mash temperature up to 55°C. Let it stand for half an hour and then raise the temperature again up to 66°C. Leave for 1½ hours, occasionally returning the temperature back to this value.

2. Contain the mashed grain in a large grain bag to retrieve the sweet wort. Using slightly hotter water than the mash, rinse the grains to collect 4 gallons (20 litres) of extract.

3. Boil the extract with the first quota of hops for 1½ hours. Pitch in the Irish Moss as directed on the instructions.

4. Switch off the heat, stir in the second batch of hops and allow them to soak for 15 minutes. Strain off the clear wort into a fermenting bin and top up to the final quantity with cold water.

5. When cool to room temperature add the yeast. Ferment in a cool place until the specific gravity falls to 1012 and rack into gallon jars or a secondary fermentation vessel, fitted with an airlock. Apportion Gelatine finings before fitting airlocks.

6. Leave for 21 days before racking the beer from the sediment into primed beer bottles. Allow 24 days maturation before sampling.

Economy Mash Tun

Mashing using a 3 gallon bucket with tap and internal grain bag to contain the grain. The bucket is then placed in a home made insulated chest to conserve the heat.

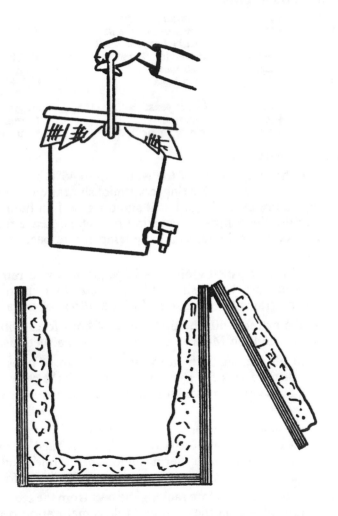

POLAND
ZYWIEC TATRA

Pronounced 'jeu-vee-etts tah-tra' if you are sober, but after a few pints of this potent brew phrasing becomes a little difficult. I vaguely remember someone explaining it meant 'Mountain Life or Spirit' when translated. The hop flavour was excellent and the strength very adequate!

Stage	5 gallons	Original gravity 1052	25 litres
1	6½ lb.	Crushed lager malt	3250 gm.
1	8 oz.	Crushed wheat malt	250 gm.
1	3 gallons	Water for 'lager' brewing	15 litres
3	1 tsp.	Irish moss	5 ml.
3	2 lb.	Golden syrup	1000 gm.
3, 4	(2½ + ¼) oz.	Saaz hops	(75 + 10) gm.
5	2 oz.	Lager yeast	60 gm.
5	½ oz.	Gelatine	15 gm.
6	¼ tsp./pint	White sugar	5 ml./litre

Brewing Stages

1. Raise the temperature of the water up to 45°C and stir in the crushed malts. Stirring continuously, raise the mash temperature up to 55°C. Let it stand for half an hour and then raise the temperature again up to 66°C. Leave for 1½ hours, occasionally returning the temperature back to this value.

2. Contain the mashed grain in a large grain bag to retrieve the sweet wort. Using slightly hotter water than the mash, rinse the grains to collect 4 gallons (20 litres) of extract.

3. Boil the extract with the first quota of hops for 1½ hours. Dissolve the golden syrup in a little hot water and add this during the boil. Also pitch in the Irish Moss as directed on the instructions.

4. Switch off the heat, stir in the second batch of hops and allow them to soak for 15 minutes. Strain off the clear wort into a fermenting bin and top up to the final quantity with cold water.

5. When cool to room temperature add the yeast. Ferment in a cool place until the specific gravity falls to 1015 and rack into gallon jars or a five gallon fermenter with an airlock. Apportion gelatine finings before fitting airlocks.

6. Leave for 21 days before racking the beer from the sediment into primed beer bottles. Allow 21 days conditioning before sampling.

SINGAPORE

TIGER LAGER

The first name in beer for people, especially the armed forces, who have visited the Eastern Countries. A light lager but sweeter than most others for the gravity.

Stage	5 gallons	Original gravity 1035	25 litres
1	5 lb.	Crushed lager malt	2500 gm.
1	1 lb. 6 oz.	Flaked rice	650 gm.
1	2½ gallons	Water for 'lager' brewing	12 litres
3	1 tsp.	Irish moss	5 ml.
3	2 oz.	Hallertau hops	60 gm.
5	10	Saccharin tablets	10
5	1 oz.	Lager yeast	60 gm.
5	½ oz.	Gelatine	15 gm.
6	½ tsp./pint	White sugar	5 ml./litre

Brewing Stages

1. Raise the temperature of the water up to 45°C and stir in the crushed malt and flakes. Stirring continuously, raise the mash temperature up to 55°C. Let it stand for half an hour and then raise the temperature again up to 66°C. Leave for 1½ hours, occasionally returning the temperature back to this value.

2. Contain the mashed grain in a large grain bag to retrieve the sweet wort. Using slightly hotter water than the mash, rinse the grains to collect 4 gallons (20 litres) of extract.

3. Boil the extract with the hops for 1½ hours. Also pitch in the Irish Moss as directed on the instructions.

4. Switch off the heat, strain off the clear wort into a fermenting bin and top up to the final quantity with cold water.

5. When cool to room temperature add the yeast and saccharin tablets. Ferment in a cool place until the specific gravity falls to 1008 and rack into gallon jars or a secondary fermentation vessel, fitted with an airlock. Apportion gelatine finings before fitting airlocks.

6. Leave for 14 days before racking the beer from the sediment into primed beer bottles. Allow 21 days maturation before sampling.

154

SOUTH AFRICA

CASTLE MILK STOUT

An excellent sweet stout brewed to a traditional styled recipe for milk stouts.

Stage	4 gallons	Original gravity 1037	20 litres
1	3½ lb.	Crushed pale malt	1750 gm.
1	1 lb.	Flaked maize	500 gm.
1	7 oz.	Crushed black malt	225 gm.
1	2½ gallons	Water for 'sweet stout' brewing	12 litres
3	12 oz.	Light soft brown sugar	400 gm.
3	2½ oz.	Saaz hops	75 gm.
5	8 oz.	Lactose	250 gm.
5	2 oz.	Brewers yeast	60 gm.
6	½ tsp./pint	White sugar	5 ml./litre

Brewing Stages

1. Raise the temperature of the water up to 55°C and stir in the crushed malt and grain. Stirring continuously, raise the mash temperature up to 66°C. Leave for 1½ hours, occasionally returning the temperature back to this value.
2. Contain the mashed grain in a large grain bag to retrieve the sweet wort. Using slightly hotter water than the mash, rinse the grains to collect 4 gallons (20 litres) of extract.
3. Boil the extract with the hops for 1½ hours. Dissolve the main batch of sugar in a little hot water and add this during the boil.
4. Switch off the heat, strain off the clear wort into a fermenting bin and top up to the final quantity with cold water.
5. When cool to room temperature add the yeast and lactose dissolved in a little water. Ferment 4—5 days until the specific gravity falls to 1010 and rack into gallon jars or a five gallon fermenter with an airlock, and fit airlocks.
6. Leave for 7 days before racking the beer from the sediment into primed beer bottles. Allow 10 days conditioning before sampling.

SOUTH AFRICA

LION ALE

A strong sweetish bitter brew with a lovely hop flavour.

Stage	5 gallons	Original gravity 1046	25 litres
1	5 lb.	Crushed pale malt	2500 gm.
1	1 lb. 5 oz.	Flaked maize	650 gm.
1	3 gallons	Water for 'bitter' brewing	15 litres
3	1 tsp.	Irish moss	5 ml.
3	1 lb. 5 oz.	Brewing sugar	650 gm.
3	2 tsp.	Brewers caramel	10 ml.
3	2 oz.	Saaz hops	60 gm.
5	5	Saccharin tablets	5
5	2 oz.	Brewers yeast	60 gm.
5	½ oz.	Gelatine	15 gm.
6	2 oz.	White sugar	60 gm.

Brewing Stages

1. Raise the temperature of the water up to 55°C and stir in the crushed malt and flakes. Stirring continuously, raise the mash temperature up to 66°C. Leave for 1½ hours, occasionally returning the temperature back to this value.
2. Contain the mashed grain in a large grain bag to retrieve the sweet wort. Using slightly hotter water than the mash, rinse the grains to collect 4 gallons (20 litres) of extract.
3. Boil the extract with the hops for 1½ hours. Dissolve the main batch of sugar and the caramel in a little hot water and add this during the boil. Pitch in the Irish Moss as directed on the instructions.
4. Switch off the heat, strain off the clear wort into a fermenting bin and top up to the final quantity with cold water.
5. When cool to room temperature add the yeast and saccharin tablets. Ferment 4–5 days until the specific gravity falls to 1010 and rack into gallon jars or a secondary fermentation vessel, fitted with an airlock. Apportion gelatine finings before fitting airlocks.
6. Leave for 7 days before racking the beer from the sediment into a primed pressure barrel. Allow 7 days conditioning before sampling.

SPAIN

SAN MIGUEL

Extremely good lager with a delicate refreshing taste. Quite a strong brew which should not be supped in excess when lazing on a hot sunny beach!

Stage	4 gallons	5.5% Alcohol	20 litres
1	½ oz.	Hallertau hops	15 gm.
1, 2	(4 + 8) pints	Water	(2 + 4) litres
2	4 lb. tin	Edme lager kit	1820 gm. Tin
2	2 lb.	Golden syrup	1000 gm.
2	½ oz.	Lager yeast	15 gm.
4	½ tsp./pint	White sugar	5 ml./litre

Brewing Stages

1. Simmer the hops in water for ten minutes and strain off the liquid into a fermenting bin.
2. Dissolve the lager kit contents and golden syrup in hot water and add this to the bin as well. Top up to the final quantity with cold water, and add the yeast.
3. Ferment until the gravity falls to 1010 and rack into gallon jars or a five gallon fermenter, and fit airlock(s).
4. Leave for 7 days before bottling in primed beer bottles and mature for 14 days before sampling.

SWITZERLAND

HURLIMANN STERNBRAU

Lightly flavoured sweetish lager.

Stage	5 gallons	Original gravity 1047	25 litres
1	6¼ lb.	Crushed lager malt	3175 gm.
1	3 gallons	Water for 'lager' brewing	15 litres
3	1 tsp.	Irish moss	5 ml.
3	2 lb.	Golden syrup	1000 gm.
3, 4	(1¾ + ¼) oz.	Saaz hops	(50 + 10) gm.
5	5	Saccharin tablets	5
5	2 oz.	Lager yeast	60 gm.
5	½ oz.	Gelatine	15 gm.
6	½ tsp./pint	White sugar	5 ml./litre

Brewing Stages

1. Raise the temperature of the water up to 45°C and stir in the crushed malt. Stirring continuously, raise the mash temperature up to 55°C. Let it stand for half an hour and then raise the temperature again up to 66°C. Leave for one hour, occasionally returning the temperature back to this value.
2. Contain the mashed grain in a large grain bag to retrieve the sweet wort. Using slightly hotter water than the mash, rinse the grains to collect 4 gallons (20 litres) of extract.
3. Boil the extract with the first quota of Saaz hops for 1½ hours. Dissolve the syrup in a little hot water and add this during the boil. Also pitch in the Irish Moss as directed on the instructions.
4. Switch off the heat, stir in the second batch of hops and allow them to soak for 15 minutes. Strain off the clear wort into a fermenting bin and top up to the final quantity with cold water.
5. When cool to room temperature add the yeast and saccharin tablets. Ferment in a cool place until the specific gravity falls to 1012 and rack into gallon jars or a secondary fermentation vessel, fitted with an airlock. Apportion gelatine finings before fitting airlocks.
6. Leave for 21 days before racking the beer from the sediment into the primed beer bottles. Allow 21 days maturation before sampling.

BEER INDEX

INDEX

GENERAL INDEX

BREWING

A
Adjuncts 15, 17
Airlocks 65
American Beers 134, 135, 136
Australian Beers 137, 138, 139, 140

B
Barley Syrup 17
Barley wine list 14
Barrels 25, 32
Beer
—dispensers 65
—glasses 65
—list 13
—of the World 133
Belgian beers 141, 142
Bottles 25
Bottling 38
Brewers yeast 20
Brewing sugar 18
Brown ale list 14
Bruheat boiler 23, 34, 35

C
Cellar language 89
Chempro SDP 22
Czechoslavakian beer 143

D
Dixie 24, 35
Draught Guinness 39
Dutch beer 148

E
Electrim boiler 25

F
Fermenting vessel 24
Flaked barley 17
—maize 17
—rice 17
Floating mash tun 34, 35
French beer 144

G
Gas injector unit 32
Gelatine 22, 29
German beers 145, 146, 147

Grain bag 25

H
Home brewing beer yeasts 20
Hops, assessing 18
Hop pellets 18
Hydrometer 24, 27

I
Ingredients 15
Invert sugar 18
Irish moss 22
Isomerised hop extract 18
Isinglass 21
Italian beer 150

K
Keg beer list 14

L
Lactose sugar 18
Lager malt grains 16
Light ale list 13
Luxembourg beer 151

M
Malt extract syrups and powders 16
Mashing methods 33

P
Pale ale list 13
Pale malt grains 16
Polish beer 153
Polythene cube (Polypin) 23
Pressure barrels 25, 32
Priming 38

R
Real ale 75
—list 13
Rehydration 21
Roasted grains 16

S
Singapore beer 154
Sodium metabisulphite 22
South African beers 155, 156
Spanish beer 157
Sparging 36, 37
Specific gravity 27

INDEX

Stout list 14
Strong ale list 14
Sugar 15, 17
Swiss beer 158

T
Toby jugs 45
Torrefied barley 17
Treatment for water 19

W
Water 18
Wheat malt 17

Y
Yeast 20
  —starter 33

Z

The Author

In a decade of brewing Dave Line probably devised and had published more recipes for beer than anyone else in the world.

Through regular monthly articles in the 'Amateur Winemaker' magazine and his definitive first book, 'The Big Book of Brewing', he was acknowledged as one of the leading experts on home brewing in the country.

People who wanted to brew the type of beer they drink in the pub but without the too familiar stigmas associated with home brew have acclaimed his methods a major breakthrough in beer quality. He made it possible to brew for the first time commercial standard beer in the home using simple equipment.

Dave who was 37, and lived in Southampton, died suddenly in 1979, leaving a widow and young son.